BICYCLE REPAIR

BICYCLE

REPAIR

MAINTENANCE AND REPAIR OF THE MODERN BICYCLE

ROB VAN DER PLAS

CYCLE PUBLISHING / VAN DER PLAS PUBLICATIONS, SAN FRANCISCO

Publisher's information:
Cycle Publishing / Van der Plas Publications
1282 7th Avenue
San Francisco, CA 94122
USA
http://www.cyclepublishing.com
E-mail: con.tact@cyclepublishing.com

Distributed or represented to the book trade by:
USA: Midpoint Trade Books, Kansas City, KS
UK: Chris Lloyd Sales and Marketing Services/Orca Book Services, Poole, Dorset
Canada: Accent Technical Publications, Cambridge, ON
Australia:Tower Books, Frenchs Forest, NSW

Cover design:
Kent Lytle, Lytle Design, Alameda, CA

Photography for text: Neil van der Plas, San Rafael, CA

Publisher's Cataloging in Publication Data:
Van der Plas, Rob. Bicycle Repair: Maintenance and repair of the modern bicycle
1. Bicycles and bicycling—handbooks and manuals.
28 cm. Bibliography: p. Includes index
I. Title: Maintenance and repair of the modern bicycle
II. Authorship
Library of Congress Control Number: 2007921650
ISBN 978-1-892495-55-6

About the Author

Rob van der Plas is a mechanical engineer with a lifelong passion for the bicycle. Having grown up in the Netherlands, and having honed his cycling and mechanical skills in England, he has lived in California since 1968. During the years since then, he has always maintained his interest in the bicycle and cycling as an activity.

Since 1974, he has been writing articles explaining technical and safety aspects of the bicycle in a variety of American, British, German, and Dutch cycling magazines, both addressing the bike trade and the general consumer markets. These articles have covered everything from riding in traffic and safe handling techniques off-road to frame construction materials and the workings of gearing, brakes, and lighting systems.

His first book appeared in 1978, and he has been writing bicycle-related books ever since, many of which were translated into other languages. His previous English-language books include *The Penguin Bicycle Handbook* (1983), *The Mountain Bike Book* (1984), *The Bicycle Repair Book* (1985), *The Bicycle Commuting Book* (1988), *Bicycle Technology* (1991), *Mountain Bike Maintenance* (1994, 2006), *Road Bike Maintenance* (1997), *How to Fix Your Bike* (1998), and *Simple Bicycle Repair* (2005).

Since 1993, he has been actively involved in the annual International Conference of Cycling History (yes, there really is such a thing). Not only has he attended each session, he has also been responsible for editing and publishing the conference proceedings.

In addition to his writing and publishing activities, he is still a regular cyclist himself, using his bike for everyday transportation, as well as for fitness and for touring. Of course, he maintains his own bicycles.

He has also been a cycling activist ever since the early days of the San Francisco Bicycle Coalition.

As one of the world's foremost experts in the field of bicycle technology, he is frequently called upon for consultation and expert witness opinions relating to bicycle patent infringement and personal injury cases.

TABLE OF CONTENTS

INTRODUCTION

The modern bicycle is a remarkably enjoyable and efficient machine. If you have chosen a bike of the type that matches your use and the size that matches your physique, it will give you many years of use. However, things do wear out, they do come loose, and they do get out of adjustment—and sometimes they break down.

That's why a bicycle needs regular maintenance and repair work. Maintenance is the work done to prevent any potential problems as much as possible before they occur, while repair is what's done to fix things if they do break down. This book covers both.

It's not a book to read from cover to cover, but more of a reference manual with some sections that are of such general importance that you should read them right away. These are Chapters 1 through 3, which deal with general subjects, while the remaining chapters of the book are best used only as needed for specific operations.

Before you read on, I should alert you to the fact that not everybody calls the various parts of the bike, and the various tools used, by the same names. What's a transmission to one is called a geartrain to another and drivetrain to a third, and what's called a wrench in the U.S. is called a spanner or a key (depending on just what kind of wrench is meant) in Britain. This book adheres primarily to the terminology and spelling conventions common in the U.S., giving alternate (mainly British) terminology in parentheses only where it might otherwise not be immediately clear what is meant.

The other general comment is that this is not a cookbook. Although I have tried to offer step-by- step instructions wherever appropriate, you will be expected to look out for peculiarities of the bike you're working on. Yes, various bikes and their components have many things in common, but no, they're not identical. So you will have to make whatever adaptations it takes to apply the general instructions to your specific situation.

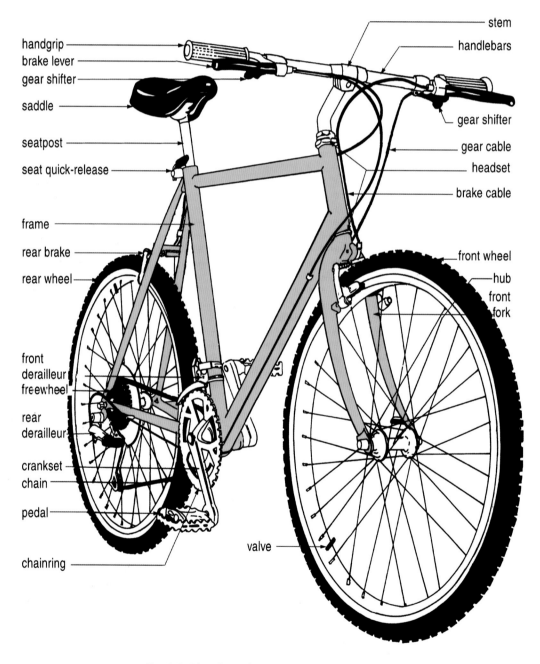

handgrip

brake lever

gear shifter

saddle

seatpost

seat quick-release

frame

rear brake

rear wheel

front
derailleur

freewheel

rear
derailleur

crankset

chain

pedal

chainring

stem

handlebars

gear shifter

gear cable

headset

brake cable

front wheel

hub

front
fork

valve

Fig. 1.1. Identifying the components of the bicycle.

1

KNOW YOUR BICYCLE

The bicycle has evolved quite a bit in recent years. The average bike today is lighter, easier to operate, and simply works better than the bikes of just two decades ago. Today, even relatively cheap machines can be a pleasure to ride.

PARTS OF THE BICYCLE

Before getting down to the actual maintenance and repair instruc-

tions, you should familiarize yourself with the bike and its components. That way it will be easier to evaluate and fix any problems once you know what the various parts are called, how they operate, and how they interact with one-another. That's what this chapter aims to explain, and to do so, I will "walk" you through the various functional component groups of the bike, explaining their operation along the way.

Of course, not all bikes are created equal, and some of the components may differ from one

model to the next. In this book, most of the illustrations and instructions will be based on "standard" derailleur bicycles, primarily the mountain bike and the road bike. However, there are many other bikes as well, ranging from comfort bikes to recumbent bicycles, and from folding bikes to tandems. Wherever the maintenance of these different machines varies significantly from

Left: Fig. 1.2. Typical mountain bike with front suspension, this one also equipped with disk brakes.

Right: Fig. 1.3. Typical road bike.

that of the more common types of bikes, model-specific instructions will be provided as much as practical.

If you bought your bike new recently, it probably came with a user's manual that contains helpful information, both with respect to handling the bike and in regards to its maintenance. Be alert for differences between your particular bike and the details described in such a manual, though, because it's probably not written quite so specifically that all of it applies to the particular model you're dealing with.

There may also have been pull tags and/or instruction manuals for some of the components and accessories installed. Keep all these instructions together for reference when you experience problems with those specific parts.

Fig. 1.1 on page 10 shows a typical bicycle with the names of the various components. Most of the same components can be found on any bike—though

sometimes in a different form or mounted in a different location. To ease the process of describing these many parts, I will treat them in "functional groups" as follows:

- frame
- wheels
- brakes
- gearing system
- drivetrain
- steering system
- saddle and seatpost
- suspension
- accessories

In Chapters 4 through 25, the individual maintenance and repair instructions will be treated, arranged roughly on the basis of these same functional groups.

THE FRAME

Together with the front fork, the frame forms the frameset. They can be considered the bike's backbone—the structure to which all the other components are at-

tached, either directly or indirectly. Although different materials (which in turn allow for frames of different shapes) may be used on some bikes, most frames still comprise a tubular metal structure as shown in Fig. 1.6.

The front part, called main frame, consists of top tube, seat tube, downtube, and head tube. The rear part, referred to as rear triangle, comprises thinner tubes, called seatstays and chainstays.

Smaller parts are attached to the various tubes to hold other components of the bicycle:

Left: Fig. 1.4.
Full-suspension mountain bike.

Top right: Fig. 1.5. Modern city bike, equipped with suspension seatpost, fenders, racks, and lights.

Bottom right: Fig. 1.6. Frame.

drop-outs, or fork-ends, to hold the wheels; brake bosses to hold the rear brake; seat clamp to hold the saddle; and the bottom bracket shell to hold the bearings for the cranks. The bearings for the steering system are installed in the head tube.

The frame is not really a candidate for maintenance and repair work very often, but Chapter 21 deals with what may be required.

THE WHEELS

After the frame, the wheels are the most critical part of the bicycle. Because they are also the most trouble-prone, they will be covered first in Chapters 4, 5, 6, 7, and 8.

Each wheel, shown in Fig. 1.7, consists of a hub and a network of spokes connecting it to the rim, on which the tire and the inner tube are mounted. The hub runs on ball bearings and is held in at the fork-ends at the front fork or dropouts at the rear triangle of the frame.

The tire is inflated by means of a valve that protrudes inward through the rim. Most wheels are held in by means of a quick-release mechanism, although on many simpler bikes they are held in with hexagonal axle nuts.

Top left: Fig. 1.7. The wheel.

Bottom left: Fig. 1.8. Hybrid bike.

Top right: Fig. 1.9. Rim brake and controls.

Below: Fig. 1.10. Tandem bicycle.

THE BRAKES

Most bicycles are equipped with one form of hand-operated rim brake or another. All these stop the bike by pushing a pair of brake pads against the sides of the wheel rim.

The brakes themselves are attached to the fork and the frame's rear triangle. Each brake is controlled by means of a lever mounted on the handlebars—one on the right, usually for the rear brake, and one on the left, usually for the front brake. A flexi-

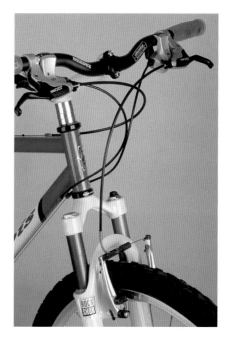

ble cable connects the lever with the brake itself. Fig. 1.9 shows a typical rim brake with matching brake lever and control cable, as used on a mountain bike.

Some bikes use brakes that act on the hub instead of on the rim. These include the disk brakes found on some mountain bikes, drum brakes found on some city bikes and (as an auxiliary brake) on some tandems, and the coaster brakes (called backpedaling brake in Britain), found on simple cruisers. The latter are installed only on the rear wheel and are operated by means of the chain when the rider pedals backward.

Disk brakes are either operated by cables, just like rim brakes, or by means of a hydraulic system, as on cars and motorcycles. Drum brakes are generally operated via cables. Alternately, on traditional heavy-duty roadsters—rarely seen in the U.S. and Britain these days—the brakes may be operated via rigid rods with pivoted connections. Chapters 15, 16, and 17 cover work on rim, disk, and hub brakes respectively.

THE GEARING SYSTEM

The vast majority of bicycles sold these days are equipped with

Top left: Fig. 1.11. Disk brake, this one cable-operated.

Bottom left: Fig. 1.12. Folding bike.

Top right: Fig. 1.13. Derailleur gearing drivetrain.

Bottom right: Fig. 1.14. Dutch city bike, equipped to handle any kind of weather.

derailleur gearing, and that's what Chapter 9 is devoted to, while Chapter 10 deals with the less common hub gearing used on some city bikes.

The derailleur system achieves changes of gear ratio, needed to adapt the rider's effort and pedaling speed to differences in terrain conditions, by moving the chain from one combination of front chainring and rear cog to another. Selecting a bigger chainring in the front or a smaller cog in the back results in a higher gear, e.g. for fast riding on a level road; selecting a smaller chainring or a larger cog provides a lower gear, e.g. for riding uphill. The number of available gears is calculated by multiplying the number of chainrings on the front by the number

of cogs in the back—usually 3 x 9 = 27 for mountain bikes and 2 x 10 = 20 for road bikes.

These "chain-derailing" operations are carried out by means of the front and rear derailleurs respectively (the one on the front is more commonly called changer in the U.K., where the rear derailleur may be referred to as "mech," short for mechanism).

The derailleurs are operated by means of shifters, which are usually installed on the handlebars, although on older road bikes, they may be found on the frame's downtube. On modern road bikes, these shifters are generally integrated with the brake levers, making for convenient shifting—but expensive repair or replacement if there is a problem. In all cases, the front derailleur is controlled from the left-side shifter, while the rear derailleur is controlled from the shifter on the right. The shifters are connected with the derailleur mechanisms by means of flexible cables.

In the case of hub gearing, shown in Fig. 1.15, gear changes are achieved by means of a kind of gear box integrated in the rear

wheel hub, although there is also a version that is connected with the front chainring and the cranks—mainly used on recumbent bicycles and on some downhill mountain bikes to replace the front derailleur.

Hub gear systems are operated by a single shifter, installed on the handlebars, via a flexible cable. Whereas derailleur gearing usually has a large number of (slightly) different gears, hub gears are generally limited to 7 or 8 speeds.

Despite the smaller number of gears, these devices usually have a range that may be quite adequate for most riding conditions short of loaded touring and out-and-out mountain bike riding.

THE DRIVETRAIN

Also known as the transmission, this is the group of components that transfers the rider's input to the rear wheel. Because the gearing system was dealt with in the previous section, this discussion will not include the parts involved in changing gears.

What will be covered here are the cranks, held at the frame's

lowest point by means of the bearings of the bottom bracket, the pedals, the chain, the chainrings (the large gear wheels attached to the right-side crank), and the cogs, or sprockets (the smaller gear wheels attached to the rear wheel hub), as well as the freewheel mechanism built into or attached to the rear wheel hub. Chapters 11, 12, 13, and 14 deal with the various components of the drivetrain.

THE STEERING SYSTEM

The steering system is quite critical not only for riding in curves and following a straight course, but also for balancing the bike. It comprises the front fork, which holds the front wheel; the handlebars; the stem, which connects these two parts; and the headset, which allows the entire system to pivot in the frame's head tube.

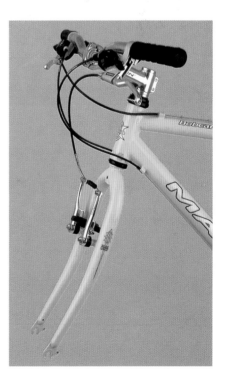

Left: Fig. 1.15.
Drivetrain on bike with hub gearing.

Right: Fig. 1.16.
Steering system.

Maintenance of handlebars, stem, and headset is covered in Chapters 18 and 19 respectively, while the fork is also dealt with in Chapter 21 (together with the frame) and in Chapter 22 (for suspension forks).

SADDLE & SEATPOST

Although perhaps the least glamorous part of the bicycle, the saddle, or seat, is not only important for comfort, but also for control of the bike. It is held in place in the

frame's seat tube by means of a seatpost, which is clamped in by means of a binder bolt. Chapter 20 deals with these components.

SUSPENSION

Many modern bikes come with some form of suspension. That may range from a simple suspension seatpost and/or a flexible handlebar stem to a complex system with telescoping front forks and a multi-linkage rear suspension. Although they were first widely applied to mountain bikes, they are now also penetrating the hybrid and city bike market. Chapters 22 and 23 deal with front and rear suspension-related problems respectively.

LIGHTING

Chapter 24 is devoted to lighting equipment, both battery-powered and generator-powered, both of which systems have seen enough progress in recent years to justify a chapter devoted to their maintenance issues.

OTHER ACCESSORIES

Although none are shown in Fig. 1.1, there is a wide range of accessories available for the bicycle. A lot of more or less useful items are available to attach to the bike. They range from high-tech to very simple, and from very important to trivial—which in turn depends on the circumstances of the bike's use. Such items as locks, reflectors, bicycle computers, luggage racks (carriers), and fenders (mudguards) are covered in Chapter 25.

Finally, the tools to use for the various maintenance and repair jobs are covered in the Appendix.

Top Left: Fig. 1.17. Front suspension.

Bottom left: Fig. 1.18. Rear suspension.

Top right: Fig. 1.19. Seat and seatpost.

Bottom right: Fig. 1.20. Same bike, different sizes.

2 BASIC MAINTENANCE PROCEDURES

Many of the jobs to be done on the bike involve work on a small number of common parts or systems: screw threaded connections, quick-release mechanisms, cable controls, and ball bearings.

COMMON PROCEDURES

To avoid the need to explain such common principles for each repair or maintenance procedure where they apply, they have been summarized in this chapter. This way, you will be familiar with their operation, so the actual instructions in the rest of the book can be kept manageably brief.

EQUIPPING YOUR WORKSHOP

It's nice to have a designated bike workshop, but it's easy enough to improvise in a small area. Although I now have a nicely equipped workshop in my house, I have at times set up provisional

Left: Fig. 2.1. Fully equipped home bike workshop.

Below: Fig. 2.2. Bike held on shop stand.

Right: Fig. 2.3. Bike on repair stand and clamping detail.

workshops in places as diverse as the corner of my bedroom and the kitchen of a small apartment. All you need is an area at least 7 feet (2.10 m) long and 5 feet (1.50 m) wide. By way of equipment, you will need a work stand (or some home-spun arrangement to hold the bike steady, preferably with the wheels off the ground) and a workbench. If you don't have a real workbench, a folding contraption such as a Workmate, or even an old piece of sturdily supported kitchen counter, 3 feet (90 cm) wide and 2 feet (60 cm) deep, will suffice.

As for the tools, I prefer to have them accessible on a board hung along a wall, but if you don't have room for that, you can keep them in a large tool box. If you hang them on a board on the wall, experiment with the most economic layout (placing the most frequently used tools near the bottom in the middle of the board) with the board lying flat down, then trace the tools' outlines with a bold marker, and install the hooks to hang the tools from, before installing the board on the wall. That way you'll always know which tools are

missing from the board and where to hang them back.

Place items such as lubricants, solvents and cleaning materials on a shelf along one of the walls, and hang some small bins (no bigger than a shoe carton) above each other for spare parts, cleaning cloths, and items to be cleaned, repaired, replaced, or discarded.

You'll need a light over the work bench and at least one over the bike. In addition, I suggest getting a drop light and putting a number of hooks in the ceiling to hang it from in different places, as you may need it to shed more light on a particular part of the bike.

The bike itself is best supported on a commercially available work stand. However, bikes with flat handlebars can often be worked on by merely turning them upside-down (but turn anything mounted on the handlebars out of the way first). It is also possible to put the bike on a simple shop display stand, supporting it near the bottom bracket. Finally, you can make a simple contraption to hang the bike

from the ceiling, supported at two points.

SPARES & REPLACEMENT PARTS

If you find that any parts are seriously damaged or worn, they have to be replaced. For some items, you should actually have spares available. A spare tube is essential, as is a spare battery and light bulbs if you ride at night. In your home workshop, you may decide to keep a store of other minor parts as well. Just what to stock depends on how much work you find yourself doing on the bike, and only your own experience after a season's work will tell you what to keep around.

Whenever you buy spares or replacement parts, take your bike to the bike shop with you (and if you can't take the whole bike, at least take the part to be replaced and the part to which it is connected), to be sure you get something that doesn't just look like it, but something that actually fits properly. For the same reason, I suggest you make a list of the make and model information for all the components installed on the bike.

I also recommend you try finding a bike shop where the owner and the mechanics are cooperative in advising you on work you want to do yourself, and take the time to make sure you get the right parts and tools. Then stay with that shop as much as possible.

Left: Fig. 2.4. Most bikes can also be worked on when turned upside-down, resting on handlebars and saddle.

GENERAL OVERHAULING PROCEDURES

In the course of your work on the bike and the individual components, you'll often have to remove parts or disassemble them. If you don't go about that work systematically, you may end up with a bunch of little bits and pieces that you can't figure out how to put together again. To make your work easier, proceed as follows:

1. Select a container big enough to hold all the main parts of the item you'll be working on, and a smaller one for the small parts (on small components, you'll need only the smaller one, and a pie dish is about ideal). When taking things apart, clean and inspect each item, big or small, as you remove it and place it in the appropriate container, if at all possible, line them up in the sequence in which they were installed.

2. When disassembling a particular component, such as a brake or a pedal, it's not always necessary to remove the entire part off the bike first. Check out the situation first and decide whether it will be easier to work on it when still on the bike or when removed in its entirety.

   • If you remove a part off the bike, first detach any controls, such as cables, then locate the main mounting bolt or bolts and remove it (or them).

   • If you work with the part still on the bike, only undo those connections that would interfere with your disassembly work.

3. Work systematically, disassembling all the components in one sub-component at a time and keeping all the pertinent parts together. For each item you remove, establish whether it is still in good condition and, if necessary, make a note to replace anything that is seriously worn or broken.

4. When everything has been taken apart, give the components a more thorough cleaning, still keeping them together and in sequence, as much as possible.

5. Also clean the portion of the bike where the part was installed, as well as the part(s) that you do not remove from the bike.

6. Except for parts made of natural rubber, lightly coat each component with lubricant or wax (wax for larger parts, oil for all small and hidden parts, especially those that move during operation).

7. Start reassembly working just as systematically as the disassembly process, checking for each part you assemble whether it fits properly on the other parts already installed.

8. Once completely reassembled and installed on the bike, make any necessary hookups, such as control cables. Wipe off any excess lubricant and test the component and all its parts for proper operation. Make any adjustment necessary.

DEALING WITH INSTRUCTIONS

Wherever practical, the advice in this book is cloaked in terms of step-by-step instructions. However, usually things are not as straightforward as this method suggests. There are always variations to the way components of the bike are made and assembled; different manufacturers insert extra parts to take up extra space one way or the other; what's usually screwed on may be held in a different way on one model or another. So the message is that, although you can take these procedures as pretty good general guidelines, Don't be surprised if one detail or an other doesn't go together quite as described.

Be observant when adjusting components, checking their function and condition, and when taking them apart or reassembling them. You can usually figure out between the descriptions and the actual situation as found on your bike just how the particular variant in question should be installed or operated.

If you can't figure it out yourself, take your bike to a bike shop and ask for advice. Sometimes it will be better to have them do the work in question, especially if it requires special tools that are too expensive, considering how rarely you would need them. However, if the people at the bike shop do not encourage you to work on your bike yourself at all, I suggest you find another one with a more encouraging staff.

In addition to the instructions in this book, it will be a good idea to consult the owner's manual and/or the manuals for specific components of your bike. They often contain useful maintenance instructions that relate specifically to the components and/or accessories installed on your particular bike.

SCREW-THREADED CONNECTIONS

Most of the parts on your bicycle are connected by means of screwed connections. This applies not only to common nuts and bolts but also to more intricate components. The principle

of screw-thread connections, simple though it seems, bears some explanation in order to manipulate them correctly. Three functions are involved: tightening, loosening, and adjusting.

All screw-threaded connections comprise a cylindrical part with a helical groove cut around the circumference (referred to as the male part, which can be e.g. a bolt or an axle) and a hollow part with a matching groove cut around the inside of the circular hole (referred to as the female part, which may be e.g. a nut).

When turning the male part relative to the female one (or vice versa, which has the same effect), the male part enters the female one further or less far, depending on which direction it is turned. If it enters further when turning clockwise, the system has right-hand thread, which is common for all regular nuts and bolts; if it enters further when turning counterclockwise, it has left-hand thread, which is used in a few places, e.g. on the left-side pedal.

Usually, there is a washer (a metal ring) between the female part and any other part that is clamped or screwed in underneath. This is to reduce the friction and make it easier to tighten and loosen the connection (thus indirectly increasing the effectiveness of the connection). Sometimes the washer takes the form of a spring washer (e.g. on minor accessories that might otherwise come loose under vibration). In other cases the washer is "keyed," which means it can only be inserted in a specific orientation (especially between screwed parts of adjustable ball bearings, to allow tightening the one part without affecting the adjustment of the other part).

To tighten a screw-threaded connection, turn one of the parts clockwise relative to the other (assuming it has right-hand screw thread; counterclockwise in the case of left-hand screw thread) until it butts up against the component that is to be secured. If all is well, the resistance when turning the parts relative to each other is quite low up to this point and will suddenly increase. At this stage, the two helical grooves are being pushed relative

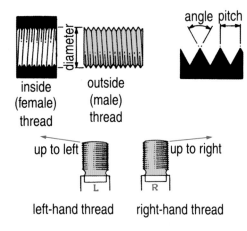

Fig. 2.5. Screw thread details.

Right: Fig. 2.6. In addition to nuts and bolts, many other parts on the bike are connected and/or adjusted by means of screw thread.

to each other and the end surfaces of the components rub against each other, until the force between them is so great that the connection becomes firm.

The characteristic by which screw-threaded components are identified is the outside diameter of the male part, measured in mm for metric components. Even though the diameter of two threaded connections may be the same, there are other aspects in which they can differ. In addition to the question of right- or left-handed thread, there may be a difference in pitch (measured as the distance between consecutive grooves on the male part), and there may be a difference in the angle of the groove. The latter is not an issue for most minor items, but can matter when matching more delicate items such as crankset and headset bearing parts.

When replacing bolts and nuts, be careful to use only metric ones. In some sizes, it is hard to tell metric and non-metric nuts and bolts apart (e.g. in the 5 mm size, which is deceptively similar to $3/16$ inch) and would ruin the components due to the difference in thread pattern. The way to check if they're not marked accordingly (e.g. on the head of a bolt) is by means of a thread gauge, lining it up with the thread with the "saw-tooth" pattern of the gauge.

To loosen the connection, turn the part in the opposite direction, which at first requires force to overcome the resistance of the end surfaces, before the situation is reached where the re-

sistance becomes much less when merely adjusting the position of the two parts relative to each other. What holds the connection in place when fastened is the force between the helical grooves when tightened, and any other forces should be minimized to reach this force. A connection will not hold as reliably if you feel great resistance all the way due to dirt, damage, or corrosion of threads or other surfaces. Therefore, it is easiest to tighten or loosen a connection with clean and corrosion-free screw threads and end surfaces, slight lubrication, and the use of a smooth, hard-surfaced washer between the end surfaces.

To tighten or loosen a screwed connection, one part has to be turned in the appropriate direction with a precisely fitting tool with enough leverage, such as a wrench while the other part must be held steady. In the case of a nut-and-bolt connection, you'll need to hold the nut with a wrench, while in the case of something screwed directly into the bicycle frame, you can hold the frame by hand or under the force of a work stand.

If you have difficulty loosening a connection that's been in place for a long time, spray some penetrating oil (e.g. WD-40) at the point where the male part engages the female, and wait 2–3 minutes before trying again.

When reinstalling screwed connections, make sure they are clean, undamaged, and not corroded—and clean, lubricate, and/or replace them with new parts if they are not. Always use a

smooth washer under the head of any bolt or nut.

Regular bolts come in a variety of head shapes. These days, the Allen head screw has become quite prevalent on bicycles, and it is indeed the most elegant, also because the hexagonal recess and the matching tool seem to experience much less damage than the older flat screw cut and the hexagonal bolt head. There's also the so-called grub screw (worm screw in Britain), which doesn't have a head at all—it can disappear completely into the female part. Nowadays, these usually have a (small) hexagonal recess in the end so they can be adjusted with an Allen wrench, whereas older ones are adjusted with a screwdriver.

To prevent accidental loosening of screwed connections, there are a number of different solutions. On many parts a double set of nuts is used, a thin so-called locknut and a regular nut, which are tightened against each other for a more effective hold. In fact, even a single nut may serve that same purpose if the bolt is screwed into a threaded hole of the part and then a nut is screwed on from the other side to lock it in place. In such cases (e.g. the pivot bolts on a dual-pivot brake), always

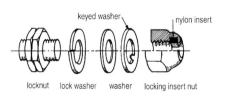

Fig. 2.7. Screw-tread locking devices.

disassemble by first removing the nut, then the bolt. Assemble by first screwing in the bolt until the pivot feels just right, then screw on the nut while holding the bolt.

Nuts used on screws and bolts for accessories are often equipped with a spring washer, or lock washer, between the accessory and the nut to take up vibrating motions without loosening. More effective than the lock washer is the locking insert nut, in which a little nylon insert gets deformed around the screw thread and pushes in firmly enough to stop the nut from coming loose. Accessories should always be held with a minimum of two screws or bolts in order to minimize the effect of the unsupported mass that would cause parts to vibrate loose if held in only one spot.

When tightening threaded connections, do not apply more torque than required—to avoid damaging the head of the bolt or some other part. For this reason, choose tools of a length that's commensurate with the part in

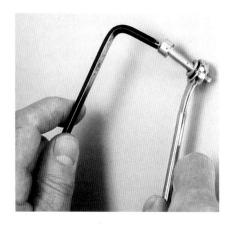

Above: Fig. 2.8. Use a tool on both sides of a screw-threaded connection to loosen, tighten, or adjust it.

question. A 5 mm bolt or nut should not be handled with a 10-inch long adjustable wrench but with a small one (and preferably with a fixed rather than an adjustable wrench), which will have an appropriate length. Ideal would be to use a torque wrench on all connections, but for most components it is not so easy to find out just how much torque is appropriate. Choosing moderate size tools is usually quite adequate.

Especially large aluminum screw-threaded components should be handled with great care to avoid damage to the screw thread. For this reason, use only the specific tools made for these components.

When screw-threaded connections are used for adjustment, there will be one male and two female components, and the latter two are tightened against each other once the correct adjustment has been established. Since this is most commonly done in the case of adjustable ball bearings on the bike, this will be described in detail under *Ball Bearings* on page 26.

QUICK-RELEASE MECHANISMS

These devices are most frequently used on the wheels to allow easy removal and installation of the wheels. The same principle of operation is also found on many brakes, in order to open them up far enough for easy wheel removal, and on the clamp that holds the seat to facilitate easy

seat height adjustment. They all work on the same principle, which involves a cam-shaped device connected to a lever that can be partially rotated to tighten or loosen a connection. In most cases, the cam is hidden inside some other part, so it's hard to figure out how it works without a drawing.

When the lever is in the "open" position, the small end of the cam is engaged, leaving the connection loose. When the lever is placed in the "closed" position, the long end of the cam is pushed just past the engagement point (the tension being at its highest when the high point of the cam was engaged), which ensures that the tension is high enough but enough force would have to be applied to move it back to the "open" position to prevent accidental opening.

If the lever is not marked with the words "open" and "close," you can still tell which is which by observing what happens when you move the lever from one position to the other. Most modern levers are shaped with a convex (bulged) surface that faces out when closed and a concave (cupped) surfaces showing when open.

In all cases, once the adjustment is correct, the secret is to

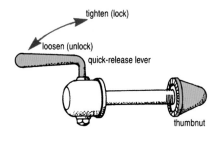

Fig. 2.9. Quick-release operation.

operate only the lever and not the nut or other device with which the pre-tension of the mechanism can be adjusted, which should be left alone whenever possible. Unfortunately, the recent trend to equip the tips of front forks of bicycles with ridges makes it impossible to use the quick-release mechanism of the hub the way it was intended. You can, of course, still loosen and tighten the mechanism properly just using the lever, but the ridges on the ends of the fork blades require loosening the thumb nut at the other side to provide enough clearance to slip over these ridges to remove or install the wheel.

These ridges are being provided to prevent accidental wheel disengagement due to liability problems (that's why they're sometimes referred to as "lawyers lips"). However, when handled properly, there is no risk of accidental wheel disengagement even on forks without these ridges.

Initial adjustment of the quick-release mechanism is done when the bike is assembled in the factory or the bike shop, but

you will probably have to do it again at some point later on after wear and tear or other factors have affected the adjustment. Proceed as follows:

QUICK-RELEASE HANDLING PROCEDURE:

1. Set the lever in the "open" position.

2. Place the device (wheel, brake, seatpost) in position. If it can't be done, loosen the thumb nut at the other end far enough until things fit.

3. Place the item to be held in the exact position and orientation it should be.

4. Screw in the thumb nut until all slack is taken up, but don't forcibly tighten it.

Above: Fig. 2.11. Tightening the quick-release lever.

Left: Fig. 2.10. When installing or removing, the quick-release must be in the "open" position.

5. Flip the lever over into the "closed" position, if possible—if it cannot be moved fully into the "closed" position, unscrew the locknut in half-turn increments until it can be closed with firm hand force.

6. Check once more whether the device is aligned properly and loosen, then re-tighten it if necessary.

CABLE CONTROLS

Flexible cable controls are commonly used on the bicycle to operate hand brakes and gear shifting devices. They're often referred to as "Bowden cables" after their inventor.

It combines a flexible, stranded inner cable, or wire, to take up tension forces, with a flexible but non-compressible wound spiral outer cover, or sleeve, to take up compression forces. The ends of the outer cover are restrained in fixed cup-shaped attachments, while the inner wire has a soldered or crimped-on nipple at one end and is clamped in at the other end.

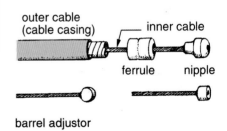

Fig. 2.12. Control cable details.

In some cases, the cables are sold only as matched sets in a length that is specific to a particular make and model, e.g. in the case of many modern gear-change mechanisms. Otherwise, you can just buy the outer sleeve by the foot or the meter and buy the inner cable in sections long enough to match any application (just make sure the nipple has the right shape and the cable has the same diameter as the original cable used).

To prevent corrosion, apply some lubricant between the inner cable and the outer sleeve. When installing a cable, run the inner cable through a wax-soaked cloth. Later, you can apply just a little oil from a spray can of lubricant at the points where the inner wire disappears into the outer sleeve whenever you do regular maintenance.

The tension of any control cable is adjusted by means of a barrel adjuster, which works in conjunction with the clamping attachment for the inner cable. Although you can usually adjust the system adequately just using this device, you may at times have to undo the clamping nut or screw and clamp the cable in at a slightly different point.

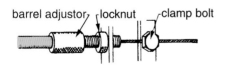

Fig. 2.13. Cable adjuster and clamping-in detail.

CABLE ADJUSTING PROCEDURE:

1. Check to make sure any quick-release device that may be provided in the system is tensioned, and if not, tension it.

2. Verify whether it's still "out of adjustment" once the quick-release is set properly. If not, proceed to Step 3.

3. Loosen the locknut by several turns, which can usually be done by hand, without the need for a tool.

4. Turn the adjusting barrel out relative to the part into which it is screwed (to increase) or in (to reduce) the tension on the cable. Loosening will open up the brake or make the derailleur shift later; tightening will do the opposite.

5. Holding the adjusting barrel with one hand, tighten the locknut again.

6. Check to make sure the mechanism is adjusted as intended. If not, repeat until it is.

NOTE:

On many newer road bikes, there is an adjuster without a locknut installed on one of the brake levers or on the derailleur. In that case, instead of following Steps 3 through 5, merely turn the adjuster out or in to achieve tightening or loosening respectively. In case of the brakes, this only works properly if you first undo the brake quick-release—and don't forget to tension it again afterward.

If the adjustment cannot be achieved this way, the end of the cable must be clamped in at a different point—further in to tighten, out to loosen the cable.

CABLE CLAMPING PROCEDURE:

1. First release tension on the cable—either using the quick-release device, if provided, or at the barrel adjuster per Steps 3 and 4 of the *Cable adjusting procedure*.

2. Loosen the clamp nut or bolt that holds the end of the cable.

3. Using needle-nose pliers, pull the cable into the appropriate position—usually no more than ¼ inch (6 mm) from its original clamping position.

Above: Fig. 2.14. Typical modern control cable adjuster.

4. While holding the cable in place with the pliers, tighten the clamp bolt firmly.

5. Carry out an adjustment as described above, using the barrel adjuster.

Cable friction can be minimized (improving operation of the brakes or the gears) by keeping the outer sleeve as short as possible, providing the radius of any curves in the cable is at least 10 times the diameter of the outer cable (given that most cables measure about ¼ inch, or 6 mm, they can be routed with a curve radius as tight as 2.5 inches, or 6 cm). However, you may find routing them just a little less tightly

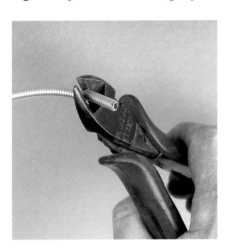

"looks" better and that's OK too—within reason.

Replace any cable that has broken strands, usually at one of the ends.

The most common way to prevent fraying is by installing a little cap over the end, which then gets crimped on. Remove it by pulling it off with pliers. To install a new cap, you must be careful the cable does not fray as you're trying to push it on. Then use pliers to crimp it on.

A better way to prevent frayed cables is to solder the strands of the cable together (you'll need a soldering iron and some rosin-core soldering wire, both

Above: Fig. 2.15. Crimping on cable-end ferrule.

Top left: Fig. 2.16. Cutting outer cable.

Bottom left: Fig. 2.17. Cutting inner cable using cable cutters.

Bottom right: Fig. 2.18. Soldering cable end.

readily obtainable in electronics and hardware stores). Solder the strands of the cable together before you cut the cable, right at the spot to cut.

CABLE CUTTERS

Although you can cut a control cable with diagonal cutters (see *General Tools* in the Appendix), you'll get a cleaner cut, without frayed cable strands, by using these special cable cutters for the inner cable.

BALL BEARINGS

One of the reasons the bicycle is such an efficient vehicle is the

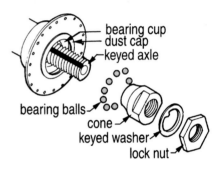

Fig. 2.19. Adjustable ("cup-and-cone") ball bearing.

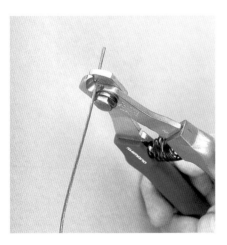

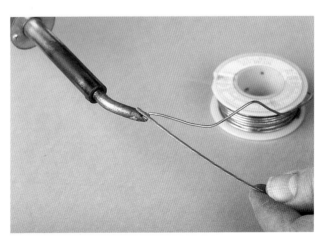

VAN DER PLAS: BICYCLE REPAIR

widespread use of ball bearings. They're everywhere on the bike: wheels, pedals, cranks, headset, and freewheel mechanism. This section deals with their function and maintenance.

First off, two different types of ball bearings are in use on the bike: adjustable and non-adjustable ones, the latter usually referred to as sealed bearings. Actually, those "sealed" bearings are not really fully sealed either, and a more accurate description would be either machine bearings or cartridge bearings, the latter being the term used elsewhere in this book.

The conventional adjustable bearing, also called cup-and-cone bearing, consists of a cup-shaped bearing race and a cone-shaped one, between which the bearing balls are contained—either loosely or held in a retainer ring—embedded in lubricant. One of the two parts (cone or cup) is adjustable by means of a screw-threaded connection, and is locked in position once it is properly adjusted by means of a lockring screwed up tightly against the screwed bearing part

with an intermediate keyed washer (stopped against rotation by means of a lip or flat section that engages a groove or flat section in the male part).

The advantage of the cup-and-cone bearing is that it can be adjusted. To do that, the cup and the cone are screwed closer together, which reduces the space for the bearing balls slightly, tightening the bearing. The disadvantage is that it is hard to seal such a bearing against the intrusion of dirt and water, possibly leading to wear and deterioration. For the manufacturer, the disadvantage is the fact that there are many loose parts, making assembly more difficult and costly.

The cartridge bearing has been the industry's answer to reduce assembly cost, but has been cleverly disguised as being more "high-tech" (which it isn't). It consists of pre-assembled non-adjustable components: an

outer bearing race, an inner bearing race, a bunch of bearing balls, held together in a retainer ring, and a set of usually neoprene (artificial rubber) seals. The disadvantage is the fact that it's not adjustable and hard to lubricate, although the advantage for the cyclist may well be less need for lubrication due to better protection against the intrusion of water and dust. When the bearing does get worn or damaged, the entire bearing assembly—the cartridge—has to be pulled off and replaced, requiring special matching tool tools.

To adjust the conventional adjustable bearing proceed as follows.

CUP-AND-CONE BEARING ADJUSTING PROCEDURE:

1. Loosen the locknut at the end of the bearing assembly.

2. Lift the keyed washer clear off the cone.

3. Turn the screwed component (usually the cone, but it may be a cup-shaped part, such as on the headset) in (to tighten)

Above: Fig. 2.20. Adjusting a cup-and-cone bearing.

Left: Fig. 2.21. Lubrication of adjustable ball bearing with bearing balls exposed.

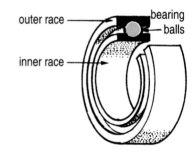

Fig. 2.22. Cartridge ("sealed") bearing.

or out (to loosen), after which the locknut.

4. Tighten the locknut again while holding the cone or the bearing race with another tool.

When you tighten the two screw-threaded parts against each other, the effect tends to be a slight tightening of the bearing; for that reason, the bearing should feel just a tiny bit loose before you do that. Even so, check to make sure the bearing is adjusted to run smoothly without noticeable play—and if not, tighten or loosen the parts a little

and repeat the operation until it is.

Lubrication, though most efficient by means of a thick mineral oil, is usually—and less messily—done with bearing grease, which gets inserted between the bearing surfaces and in which the bearing balls are embedded. Before lubricating a bearing, though, it must be thoroughly cleaned out with solvent and a clean cloth. Whatever you do, don't spray thin spray lubricant at ball bearings, because that is likely to introduce surface dirt as well as wash out any lubricant inside.

When inspecting a ball bearing, watch out for pitted and corroded surfaces—of the bearing balls or either of the bearing races (cup and cone). Replace any parts that are damaged this way, because damaged balls would rapidly start damaging the

Left: Fig. 2.23. Adjustable bearing with the cone removed.

Right: Fig. 2.24. Typical cartridge bearing hub.

other components as well, leading to loss of efficiency. When replacing bearing balls, always replace all of them, if any are visibly damaged. When taking a bearing apart, clean it out thoroughly and replace the lubricant before reassembling it.

3
PREVENTIVE MAINTENANCE

The best way to reduce the risk of accidental damage and the need for repairs is by means of regular preventive maintenance—ranging from cleaning to lubrication and adjustment of the various components. That's the subject of this chapter.

SCHEDULED MAINTENANCE

I suggest you adhere to a three-part schedule, consisting of a quick pre-ride inspection and more extensive bi-monthly and annual inspections. This way, minor problems can be fixed before they become major problems.

Just as importantly, always be alert when riding the bike, so you notice anything that may go wrong along the way, and fix such problems at the first opportunity. For instance, if you accidentally hit a pothole hard while riding, do check the condition of tire and rim afterward, and get them fixed if needed. When you do notice something is rattling, scraping, or rubbing as you ride,

find out what the cause is and correct it right away.

Finally on this subject, where you keep the bike when you're not riding it is also important for its condition. Keep it out of the rain and direct sunlight as much as possible in a place where others can't interfere with it. If you have to keep it in a public or quasi-public place—whether that's in front of your place of work or in the back yard of an apartment building, always lock it to something fixed, using a long cable that goes through the frame and the wheels. If possible, place a tarp over the bike—preferably one "tailored" for a bike, wrapped all the way around to a point close to the ground.

PRE-RIDE INSPECTION

If you take the bike out several times on the same day, that won't be necessary each time you do, but it's a good idea to follow this procedure at least for the first ride of the day.

Of course, things don't go drastically wrong overnight. However, the effect of many days of cumulative effects of vibrations while riding are best dealt with on a daily basis—if it takes 10 days of use for something to vibrate loose, you'd probably not know

Fig. 3.1. Inflating a tire with a hand pump.

to check it at the right time unless you make it a daily routine.

TOOLS & EQUIPMENT:

- Usually none required, except any tools needed to make corrections.

PROCEDURE:

1. Check the quick-releases on the wheels, saddle, and brakes to make sure they're in the closed position. The best check is to loosen them first and then re-tighten them. If they feel at all loose, or if they don't require firm force to tighten, they're adjusted too loose. In that case, set the lever in the "open" position, tighten the thumb nut by a half turn and tighten the lever again. Repeat if necessary.

2. Check operation of the brakes. They must be able to block rotation of the wheels when the levers are pulled to

within ¾ inch (2 cm) from the handlebars. Do this by pulling each of the levers in turn while pushing down and forward on the bike at the handlebars for the front brake, on the saddle for the rear brake. Adjust if necessary.

3. Check to make sure the handlebars are straight and tight. To do that, straddle the front wheel, holding it tightly between your legs, and apply force to the handlebars trying to twist them in the horizontal plane. Adjust and tighten if necessary.

4. Especially if others sometimes ride your bike too, check to make sure the saddle is at the right height for you, straight, and firmly clamped in. Adjust and tighten if not.

5. Check whether the tires are inflated properly—at least to the pressure listed on the sidewalls. In the beginning, always use a pressure gauge; after some practice, you'll be able to quickly feel by hand whether they're at least "about right."

6. Check operation of the gears by lifting the rear wheel off the ground and trying to engage each gear combination while turning the pedals. Adjust if necessary.

Left:. Fig. 3.2. Brake check.

Right: Fig. 3.3. Bottom bracket check.

7. Rotate each wheel while lifted off the ground, to check whether they turn smoothly, without interference or visible wobbling.

8. With the rear wheel lifted, turn the cranks to make sure the drive to the wheel works smoothly. Make any corrections that may be necessary.

BI-MONTHLY INSPECTION

The bi-monthly inspection consists of a more thorough check and some routine maintenance and adjusting operations. It also includes cleaning and preserving that is not necessarily due to actual use of the bike but simply to the "ravages of time."

This inspection is best done in the workshop, if you have managed to arrange for one as described in Chapter 2, whereas the daily inspection is easily done almost anywhere the bike happens to be at the time.

When carrying out this (or any other) inspection, be alert to any signs of damage in addition to those specifically mentioned here. Thus, you may find some part to be loose, cracked, or otherwise damaged. Fix or replace such items as soon as you notice them. Ask for advice at a bike shop if you're not sure whether something is serious enough to warrant replacement.

PROCEDURE:

1. CLEANING

Clean the bike and apply protective coating as described under *Cleaning the Bike* starting on page 33.

2. LUBRICATION

Lubricate the following parts:

- The chain, spraying on a special chain spray lubricant available at a bike shop.
- Brake levers, shifters, pivot points of exposed mechanisms and cable ends, using

thin spray lubricant and aiming carefully with the thin tubular nozzle extension provided.

Afterward, wipe off all excess lubricants to prevent parts of your bike becoming sticky and attracting dirt.

3. GENERAL CHECK

Follow all the steps described under *Pre-Ride Inspection* on page 28.

4. WHEEL BEARINGS

Check the wheels for loose bearings (applying sideways force at the rim while holding the front fork for the front wheel, or the frame for the rear wheel)—if it moves, the bearings have to be adjusted as per Chapters 3 and 6.

5. WHEEL RIM AND SPOKES

Check the wheels for wobble and loose, bent, or broken spokes. Wheel wobble is checked by lifting the wheel off the ground and

looking at it from behind at a fixed point while slowly rotating it. If it appears to wobble sideways or up-and down as it turns, it needs to be "trued," following the instructions in Chapter 7, which also includes instructions for dealing with loose, bent, or broken spokes.

6. TIRES AND TUBES

Check the tires for damage and significant wear. Replace them if there are bulges, cuts, or seriously worn areas. Remove any embedded objects and replace the tube if it has been losing pressure from one day to the next. Make sure the valves are seated straight and the tires are seated

Fig. 3.4. Lubrication points.

Top right: Fig. 3.5. Lubricating the front derailleur.

Bottom right: Fig. 3.6. Lubricating the chain.

equally deep all around the rims. Chapter 5 has all the relevant instructions.

7. BRAKES

Check the operation of the brakes and, if the bike has rim brakes, observe whether the brake pads (brake blocks) touch the rim squarely over their entire length and width when you pull the brake lever to within about ¾ inch (2 cm) from the handlebars. Adjust if necessary, referring to the instructions in Chapter 15.

8. CRANKS

Using either the wrench part of the crank tool or a fitting Allen wrench (depending on the crank attachment detail), tighten the bolts that hold the cranks to the bottom bracket axle. You may have to remove a dust cap first, and reinstall it to protect the internal screw thread.

9. ACCESSORY CHECK

Inspect any accessories installed on the bike, as well as any you keep at home for occasional use.

Make sure they are in operating order, and fix them if not. Tighten the mounting hardware for anything installed on the bike.

10. FINAL CHECK

Carefully go over the entire bike and check to make sure all nuts and bolts are in place and tightened, nothing is loose, and no parts are missing or damaged. Make any corrections necessary.

ANNUAL INSPECTION

This is essentially a complete overhaul, to be carried out after a year's intensive use. If you ride in really bad weather and muddy terrain a lot—like real mountain biking—I'd even encourage you to carry out this inspection twice a year, once each at the end of

Above: Fig. 3.8. Lubricating derailleur pulley bearings.

Left: Fig. 3.7. Lubricating derailleur pivot point.

Right: Fig. 3.9. Lubricating cable at derailleur.

summer and the end of winter. Proceed as outlined below.

PROCEDURE:

1. PRELIMINARY WORK

Clean the bike and then carry out all the work described above for the pre-ride inspection and the bi-monthly inspection.

2. VISUAL INSPECTION

Carefully check over the entire bike and all its components and accessories noting any damage, and correct any-thing that appears to be wrong before proceeding, following the instructions in the relevant chapters—or referring the work to a bike shop.

3. WHEELS

For each wheel (still on the bike), check all around the tire and the rim for any signs of damage or serious wear, as well as bent or broken spokes, and correct any-thing found amiss, following the instructions in Chapters 6 and 7. Then remove the wheel from the bike and overhaul the wheel hubs, referring to the instructions in

Chapter 6 (if the hubs have adjustable bearings). If the hubs have cartridge bearings, thoroughly clean the surfaces and note any signs of rough operation or looseness, in which case you should replace those bearings completely, either using a special tool or entrusting that work to a bike shop mechanic.

4. CHAIN

Remove the chain and clean it thoroughly by washing it in a container with solvent, using a brush, then letting it dry over the used solvent bath and rubbing it with a cloth. Check for apparent chain "stretch" (actually, the effect of wear). To do that, you can either use a special chain length gauge or measure the length of a 50-link section. On a new chain, that should measure 25 inches (63.7 cm), and any greater length is a sign of wear. Since 2 percent is the maximum allowable wear, replace the chain if the 50-link section measures more than 25½ inches (65 cm). Instructions for this work can be found in Chapter 13. Finally, lubricate the chain.

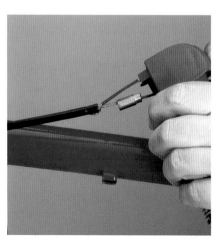

5. BOTTOM BRACKET

With the cranks still attached to the bottom bracket axle, check to make sure there is no sideways play, which would indicate loose bearings. Then remove the cranks, following the instructions in Chapter 12, and spin the bottom bracket axle to make sure it rotates smoothly. If there is any sign of wear or looseness, take the bearings apart, clean and lubricate them, and adjust them (if it's an adjustable type, done from the right side) or replace the bearings (if they're of the cartridge type). Finally, reassemble the bottom bracket and the cranks.

6. PEDALS

Turn the pedals, and check to make sure they turn freely but without play and they don't wobble as you rotate them (which

Above: Fig. 3.11. Cleaning and polishing the frame's paint.

Left: Fig. 3.10. Lubricating cable.

Right: Fig. 3.12. Cleaning and lubricating a suspension fork's stanchion tube.

would be a sign of a bent axle). If anything is not right, remove the pedals and disassemble them to clean, lubricate and adjust or replace the bearings and replace any damaged parts, following the instructions in Chapter 14.

7. STEERING

Check the operation of the headset as described for the monthly inspection. If there is any sign of looseness or rough operation, overhaul it. See the instructions for overhauling the headset in Chapter 19.

8. GEARING

While the chain is removed for the work per Step 4 above, thoroughly clean, check, and lubricate all the components of both derailleurs (if the bike has derailleur gearing), making sure the pivots operate smoothly and the little pulleys over which the chain normally runs turn freely (unlike all other rotating parts on the bike, in their case, it's normal that they have quite a bit of lateral play). Fix or replace any problem-

atic parts as explained in Chapter 9.

9. CONTROLS

Remove the control cables for both the gearing and the brakes. Clean them, replace them if there is any damage (such as broken strands or frayed ends on the inner cable, or kinks in the outer cable). Then rub wax onto the inner cable and reinstall the cables, referring to Chapters 9 and 15 for gears and brakes respectively.

While the cables are removed, inspect the shifter and the brake lever for smooth operation, at which time you will also have a better chance to clean and lubricate the moving parts of these devices.

After you have reinstalled the cables, check the operation of the system and make any adjustments that may be necessary.

10. ACCESSORIES

If you have any accessories for the bike—whether permanently installed or not—this is the time

to check their condition and operation, and take any corrective action that may be needed. Also check on any spare parts you have for the bike and/or its accessories. For example, if the spare tube you carry or keep at home has been used on the bike, make sure it is either repaired properly or replaced by a new one. Similarly, spare bulbs or batteries for a lighting system should be checked and replaced if necessary.

Finally, check the contents and condition of your tool kit and replace anything that's found wanting (e.g. the rubber solution and the patches in the tire repair kit have a limited shelf life, even if not used, and should be replaced with new ones once every two years).

CLEANING THE BIKE

Depending on what kind of terrain and weather you ride, clean

Above and left: Fig. 3.14 & 3.15. Cleaning around bottom bracket bearings.

Right: Fig. 3.13. Cleaning clipless pedal spring mechanism.

your bike more or less frequently. In fact, in serious mountain biking, that may be as often as after every such ride.

The kind of dirt that settles on the bike also determines the materials used for cleaning and protecting the bike. Where I live, in Northern California, we encounter about 7–8 months of dry, dusty conditions, and 4–5 months of possibly wet, muddy ones. During the wet period, it's important to avoid corrosion and thus necessary to use wax and lubricants rather generously. However, when it's dry and dusty, open lubricated parts are actually a hazard because of their tendency to hold fine dry dust particles that work like an abrasive, causing wear and rough operation of moving parts and controls.

Keep such points in mind while otherwise generally following the following procedure.

PROCEDURE:

1. If the bike is dry, wipe it clean as much as possible with a soft brush or a clean cloth to remove any loose dust. If the

bike is wet or the dirt is caked on, clean the bike with a bucket full of water and a sponge.

Don't use a hose with a strong spray nozzle, to avoid getting water into the bearings and other sensitive parts. After washing the frame itself, take each of the other components and thoroughly clean around them.

2. Use a clean, dry cloth to dry off all the parts that got wet in the preceding operation.

3. Next, use a solvent-soaked cloth to clean the small, hidden corners of the bike and its components and accessories—from the areas around the spokes to those behind the brakes and the nooks and crannies of the derailleurs. Many of the smallest corners are best reached by wrapping the cloth around a thin, narrow object, such as a screwdriver, while the way to get between

or behind the cogs and the chainrings is by folding the cloth and pulling it back-and-forth from both sides.

4. To protect the areas you've just cleaned under Step 3, do the same with a cloth soaked in lubricant or wax (use wax for dry weather, especially if it will be dusty, and oil if the weather and the terrain are more likely to be wet).

• You can combine Steps 4 and 5 by soaking the cloth in a mixture of solvent with about 10 percent oil.

5. Treat all painted and unpainted metal surfaces of the

Left: Fig. 3.16. Cleaning between the freewheel cogs.

Above: Fig. 3.17. Cleaning around the hub bearings.

Right: Fig. 3.18. Cleaning the front derailleur.

bike and its parts with wax. If the paint or the metal surfaces appear to be weathered, you can use an automotive liquid wax that contains an abrasive compound, otherwise regular automotive wax is the material to use. Ideally, you should remove the handlebar stem and the seatpost, so you can also treat the hidden portions of those parts.

Reinstall them at the right height and orientation, and make sure they're held in place firmly, following the instructions in Chapters 18 and 20 respectively.

6. Rub out the wax coating with a clean, dry, soft cloth.

7. Treat all non-metallic surfaces, such as plastic (but *not* natural rubber, i.e. the tires), with Armor-All or a similar material for treating plastic parts of cars. Spray it on and rub it out with a clean, dry, soft cloth.

4 WHEEL REMOVAL & INSTALLATION

Probably no other bicycle component requires more frequent maintenance than the wheels. This chapter provides detailed instruction for wheel removal and installation. Chapter 5 covers the tires, Chapter 6 the hubs, Chapter 7 rim and spokes, while Chapter 8 deals with the special subject of wheel building.

in with a quick-release or with axle nuts, and whether it's a regular wheel or one with e.g. a disk or hub brake or hub gearing. I've lumped some of these variables together in the instructions that

WHEEL REMOVAL ISSUES

Most wheel and tire problems require the wheel to be removed from the bicycle. Although this may seem like a simple task, it's an important enough one to warrant the detailed instructions given below. Actually, there are quite a number of different things to consider. It depends on many factors: whether it's a front wheel or a rear wheel, whether it's held

Left: Fig. 4.1. Wheel overview.

Top right: Fig. 4.2. Wheel with quick-release.

Bottom right: Fig. 4.3. Wheel with axle nuts ("bolted-on" wheel).

follow, leaving you with four categories: front and rear wheels, each with and without quick-release.

REPLACE FRONT WHEEL WITH QUICK-RELEASE

TOOLS & EQUIPMENT:

• Usually none required.

REMOVAL PROCEDURE:

1. Open up the brake's quick-release or cable attachment to spread the brake arms apart so the tire can pass between the brake pads (if the bike has rim brakes).

   • If there is no quick-release on the brake, you can either let the air out of the tire or undo the brake cable connection.

   • If it is a wheel with another type of brake, such as a drum brake, undo the attachment of the control cable (if any) at the brake and dislodge the coun-

ter-lever—see the instructions in Chapter 17. There are even some wheels with an electric generator, or dynamo, built into the hub, and on those you have to disconnect the electric wires.

2. Twist the hub quick-release lever into the "open" position.

3. If the front fork has ridges or some other component to stop the wheel, unscrew the thumbnut on the side opposite the lever until the hub can pass over them.

4. Slide the wheel out, guiding it at the hub and the rim.

INSTALLATION PROCEDURE:

1. If necessary, follow the same procedure as described in Step 1 above for wheel removal, so the wheel will pass between the brake pads.

2. Make sure the hub's quick-release lever is in the "open" position.

3. If there are ridges on the fork ends, unscrew the thumbnut far enough for the wheel to pass over them.

4. Slide the wheel over the fork ends, guiding it near the rim

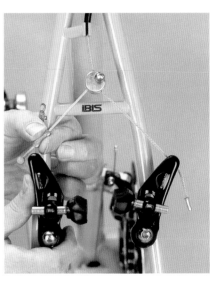

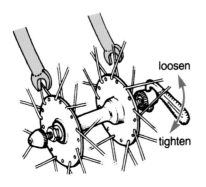

loosen

tighten

Fig. 4.4. Quick-release hub installation.

Above: Fig. 4.5. Releasing cable tension on a V-brake.

Top right: Fig. 4.6. Releasing cable tension on a sidepull brake.

Bottom right: Fig. 4.7. Releasing cable tension on a cantilever brake.

between the brake pads (if the bike has rim brakes) or at the disk for a bike with disk brakes, until the hub is seated fully at the top of the slots in the fork ends.

5. Center the wheel at the rim between the fork blades (leaving the same distance on both sides), and tighten the quick-release lever. (In case of ridges on the fork tips, first screw in the thumbnut until the lever can be tightened fully with significant hand force).

6. Redo any attachments and adjustments that were affected by the removal of the wheel (see Step 1 of the preceding *Removal procedure*).

REPLACE FRONT WHEEL WITH AXLE NUTS

Although not much used on quality bikes these days, wheels with nutted hubs available (and not inherently inferior to quick-release wheels).

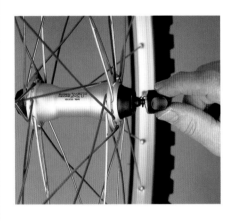

Above: Fig. 4.10. Adjusting thumb nut.

Top left: Fig. 4.8. Loosening quick-release lever.

Bottom left: Fig. 4.9. Installing wheel into fork.

Top right: Fig. 4.11. Tightening quick-release lever.

Bottom right: Fig. 4.12. This is how the conical coil springs should be oriented.

TOOLS & EQUIPMENT

• 2 wrenches to fit axle nuts

REMOVAL PROCEDURE:

1. Open up the brake's quick-release or cable attachment

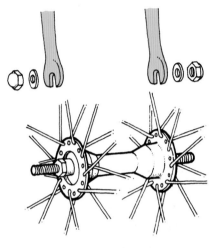

Fig. 4.13. Front hub with axle nuts.

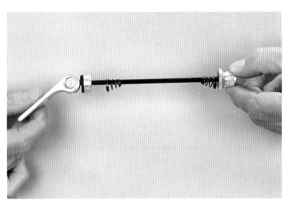

to spread the brake arms apart so the tire can pass between the brake pads (if the bike has regular rim brakes).

• If there is no quick-release on the brake, you can either let the air out of the tire or undo the brake cable connection.

• If the hub has a special brake or an electric generator built in, disconnect everything associated with it first.

2. Holding the axle nut on one side steady with one wrench, unscrew the one on the opposite side with the second wrench.

3. Unscrew the nuts far enough to slide the wheel out. If, under the washer, there is a plate with a tab that engages an extra hole in the rim, the nut must be unscrewed far enough to dislodge it. (These plates serve the same purpose as the ridges on forks for use with quick-releases, namely to avoid accidental wheel disengagement).

Fig. 4.14. Axle nuts with and without integral washer.

• If the fork blades do not have slots but round holes for the axle nuts (sometimes the case on low-end bikes), remove the nuts and washers all the way and spread the fork blades apart by hand to remove the axle ends from those holes.

4. Slide the wheel out, guiding it at the hub and the rim.

INSTALLATION PROCEDURE:

1. If necessary, follow the same procedure as described in Step 1 of the preceding *Removal procedure*, so the wheel will pass between the brake pads.

2. Make sure the washer is installed and on the outside of the fork blade, and the axle nuts are unscrewed far enough, for the little plate (if installed) to engage the

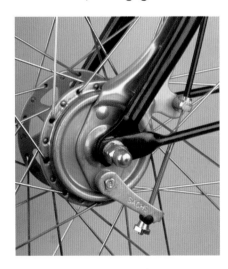

Above: Fig. 4.15. Front wheel with axle nut on a heavy-duty city bike with hub brake. Hub brakes almost invariably are equipped with axle nuts instead of quick-releases.

matching hole in the fork blade.

3. Slide the wheel into the slots in the fork ends, guiding it near the rim between the brake pads (if the bike has rim brakes) until the hub is seated fully in the slots in the fork ends.

• If the fork ends do not have slots but round holes for the axle, remove the nuts and washers all the way and spread the fork blades apart by hand to install the hub in those holes.

4. Center the wheel at the rim between the fork blades (leaving the same distance on both sides), and tighten the axle nuts—first the one side, then the other while holding the side that has been tightened.

6. Redo any attachments and adjustments that were affected by the removal of the wheel (see Step 1 of the preceding *Removal procedure*).

REPLACE REAR WHEEL WITH QUICK-RELEASE

TOOLS & EQUIPMENT:

• Usually only a cloth to keep your hands clean while manipulating the chain.

REMOVAL PROCEDURE:

1. Shift the derailleurs into the gear that engages the smallest cog in the back and the smallest chainring in the front.

2. Open up the brake's quick-release or cable attachment to spread the brake arms apart, so the tire can pass between the brake pads (if the bike has rim brakes).

 • If there is no quick-release on the brake, you can either let the air out of the tire or undo the brake cable connection.

 • If it is a wheel with a disk brake or a hub brake, undo the attachment of the control cable at the brake and dislodge the counter-lever. In case it's a wheel with a hub gear, select the highest gear and then disconnect the con-

Above: Fig. 4.16. Holding back derailleur for rear wheel removal or installation.

trol for the hub gear—see Chapter 10.

3. For derailleur gearing, hold back the derailleur with the chain as shown in Fig. 4.15 to provide a straight path, unobstructed by the routing of the chain around the derailleur pulleys.

4. Twist the hub quick-release lever into the "open" position.

5. Slide the wheel out, guiding it by the hub and at the rim.

INSTALLATION PROCEDURE:

1. If applicable, follow the instructions in Step 1 of the *Wheel removal procedure*, so the wheel will pass between the brake pads.

2. Make sure the hub's quick- release lever is set to the "open" position.

3. Make sure the chain engages the smallest chainring in the front and the rear derailleur is set for the gear in which the chain engages the smallest cog, and route the chain over that smallest cog and around the pulleys as shown in Fig. 4.17.

4. Slide the wheel into the slot in the dropouts, guiding it near the rim between the brake pads (if the bike has rim brakes).

5. Let go of the chain, routing it around the smallest cog and

the derailleur pulleys as shown in Fig. 4.17.

6. Center the wheel at the rim between the seatstays (leaving the same distance on both sides) and tighten the quick-release lever. (If it can't be tightened fully or if it is too loose, adjust the thumbnut until the lever can be tightened fully with significant hand force).

6. Redo any attachments and adjustments that were affected by the removal of the wheel (see Step 1 of the *Removal procedure*).

REPLACE REAR WHEEL WITH AXLE NUTS

Even if the bike has a quick-release on the front wheel, there may be axle nuts used in the rear.

TOOLS & EQUIPMENT:

 • 2 wrenches to fit axle nuts

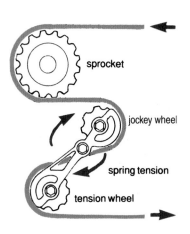

Fig. 4.17. Chain routing at rear derailleur.

- cloth to handle the chain

REMOVAL PROCEDURE:

1. Open up the brake's quick-release or cable attachment to spread the brake arms apart, so the tire can pass between the brake pads (if the bike has rim brakes).

    • If there is no quick-release on the brake, you can either let the air out of the tire or undo the brake cable connection.

    • If it is a wheel with another type of brake, such as a hub brake, undo the attachment of the control cable at the brake and dislodge the counter-lever (see Chapter 17).

    • If the bike has hub gearing, select the highest gear and disconnect the control cable at the hub (see Chapter 10).

2. Holding the axle nut on one side steady with one wrench, unscrew the nut on the opposite side with the second

wrench, then also loosen that nut.

3. For derailleur gearing, hold back the rear derailleur with the chain as shown in Fig. 4.16 to provide a straight path, unobstructed by the routing of the chain around the derailleur pulleys.

4. Slide the wheel out, guiding it at the hub and the rim.

INSTALLATION PROCEDURE:

1. If applicable, follow the same procedure as described in Step 1 above for wheel removal, so the wheel will pass between the brake pads (if the bike has regular rim brakes).

2. Make sure the washer is installed on the outside of the dropouts and the axle nuts are unscrewed far enough to fit over the dropouts.

3. Slide the wheel into the slots in the dropouts, guiding it near the rim between the brake pads (if the bike has rim brakes).

4. Let go of the chain, making sure it is routed around the smallest cog and the derailleur pulleys as shown in Fig. 4.17.

5. Center the wheel at the rim between the fork blades (leaving the same distance on both sides) and tighten the axle nuts with the wrenches—first the one side, then the other while holding the side that has been tightened with one of the two wrenches.

6. Redo any attachments and re-adjust anything that was affected by the removal of the wheel (see Step 1 of the *Removal procedure*).

SPACERS, WASHERS, & KEYED PLATES

Often, there will be one or more washers or similar items inserted between the hub and the nut or the quick-release. It's not always clear whether and where they are needed, so here's a rundown on what is and what is not needed, and where it should go.

The first step is to measure the space on the inside between the dropouts on the frame or the fork. If that dimension is more than the width of the hub between the locknuts, spacers

Left: Fig. 4.18. Installing axle nut on "bolted-on" rear wheel.

Right: Fig. 4.19. Tightening or loosening axle nut on rear wheel hub.

should be used to make up the difference, and it's best to make up half that difference on each side. Of course, those spacers go what you may call "on the inside," i.e. between the hub locknuts and the inside of the dropouts.

On the outside of hubs without quick-release, i.e. between the outside of the dropout and the axle nut, there must always be a plain washer. Don't use a spring washer, because the idea is to reduce the friction between the nut and the mating surface, so the nut can be tightened more.

Finally, there may be a keyed plate, sometimes even with an adjuster, especially on coaster brake hubs (with or without hub gears). These items serve to prevent rotation of the axle, which would ruin the effect of the brake. So the axle has flattened surfaces, and the plate has a matching hole. These plates always go on the inside, i.e. between the inside of the dropout and the hub's locknut or spacer.

Left: Fig. 4.20. Adjusting wheel positioning device.

Right: Fig. 4.21. Keyed plate to prevent axle rotation on "bolted-on" rear wheel with hub brake.

5 TIRE & TUBE MAINTENANCE

Foremost among wheel problems is the puncture, or "flat" tire. However, tires not only need work when they lose air, but there is also the need for preventive maintenance: inflating, checking for wear, and replacement of tube or tire.

TIRE TYPES

The most common type of tire is the wired-on type, usually referred to as "clincher" in the U.S. It fits around a separate inner tube and is held onto the rim by means of metal wires, or "beads" that are embedded in the sidewalls. The sidewalls are quite thin and flexible, whereas the outside surface, referred to as the tread, is thicker and usually stiffer with some kind of a pattern. That pattern, useful though it may be on a car or on a mountain bike tire, serves no sensible purpose on a road bike (due to the high contact pressure and narrow contact area between a typical bicycle tire and the road surface).

The tubes are equipped with a valve to control the air pressure. Three different valve types are in use—Presta ("French"), Schrader ("auto"), and Woods (also referred to as "Dunlop"—a type used in continental Europe, Asia, and Africa, but rarely seen in the U.S. and Britain). Make sure you get tubes with the same type of valves as the existing ones

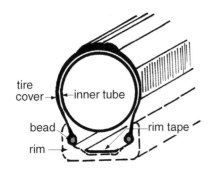

Fig. 5.1. Conventional wired-on ("clincher") tire mounted on matching rim.

Fig. 5.2. Inflating the tire, shown here with an adaptor nipple.

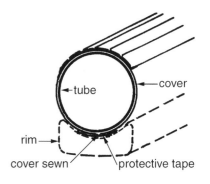

Fig. 5.3. Tubular tire ("sew-up") and matching Sprint-type rim.

on your bike (they must match the valve hole in the rim, which is smaller for the Presta valve than it is for the Schrader valve). Also make sure the pump matches that type of valve, because the use of adapter nipples is rather cumbersome.

Tires are designated by their nominal size, which can be given in one of several methods. In the U.S., the most common one reads something like 26 x 1.75, meaning the tire is approximately 26 inches in outside diameter and about 1¾ inches wide. More critical, though is the ETRTO designation, which is also provided, be it in small print, on the tire sidewall. It will read something like 559 x 47 (for the same tire), meaning it fits on a rim with a 559 mm diameter over the rim shoulder (where the bead of the tire is seated) and is 47 mm wide. Any tire with "559" in its designation will fit this rim. For road bikes, a typical size will be something like 622 x 23, meaning it fits on a 622 mm diameter rim and is 23 mm wide (this particular tire is also known as 700C x 23, although it is by no means 700 mm (28 inches) in outside diameter, but 668 mm, (i.e. not

quite 27 inches). Make sure you get tires that fit the rims and with a width that is small enough to clear the fork and the stays.

Concerning the inner tube, other than the valve type, the size is also important, though not as critical as it is for the tire cover. Check the size range for which it is recommended before you buy one. Inner tubes have a limited shelf life (they are much more sensitive to time, heat, and humidity than the tire covers seem to be), so don't buy a large supply of them at once, but rather buy just two at a time and replace them whenever you have to discard an existing tube due to age, number of patches, or porosity (when it starts losing air even though you can't identify a specific hole). They are available in different materials, and I like the very flexible ones made of "pure latex" (i.e. unvulcanized rubber) best—among other things because they are easier to patch than the ones made of butyl.

There is also a different type of tire, called "sew-up" in the U.S., "tubs" (short for "tubular tyres") in the U.K. On these tires, the inner tube is encased in the outer cover, which is sewn together, giving the whole thing the appearance of a garden hose (though much more flexible). They require special rims, to which they are glued, either directly using adhesive cement or using two-sided adhesive tape, and always come with Presta valves.

Although they are not used much anymore, their maintenance and repair are tricky enough to be covered in this chapter.

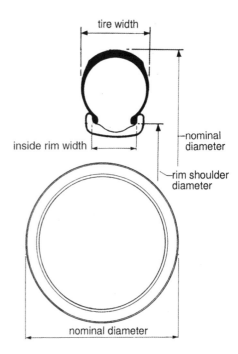

Fig. 5.6. Tire and rim dimensioning conventions.

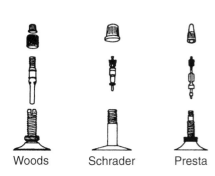

Fig. 5.4. Valve types.

Fig. 5.5. This tire cover is beyond repair and should be replaced.

TIRE INFLATION

Well, that's what's usually said, although in reality you don't inflate the tire but the tube. Inflate it whenever the pressure is inadequate, though it's usually safe to inflate to about 15 psi, or 1 bar, more or less than that figure if you prefer a harder or softer ride.

TOOLS & EQUIPMENT:

• pump

• pressure gauge, if available

PROCEDURE:

1. Make sure to use the right pump and a pressure gauge for the type of valve on the tire.

2. Check whether the valve is straight in the rim (if it isn't, let all the air out, straighten it out by manipulating the tire sidewall at the same time as the valve).

3. Remove any dust cap that may be screwed on the end of the valve.

4. Depending on the type of valve:

   • If you're dealing with a Presta valve, unscrew the little round nut at the end and briefly push in the pin in the end to which the nut is attached to loosen it, but try not to let too much air escape.

   • If the bike has a Schrader valve, briefly push in its internal pin to loosen it, but try not to let too much air escape.

5. Check the air pressure with the pressure gauge, if available (once you have enough experience, you'll have developed a "calibrated thumb" with which you can estimate the pressure reasonably accurately without such tool).

6. Place the pump head square on the valve, avoiding the escape of air; make sure it is seated properly on the valve and, if the pump has a toggle lever, flip the toggle lever that makes the pump head clamp around the valve more effectively.

7. Holding the pump under a right angle to the valve, inflate

Left: Fig. 5.7. On a Presta valve, first push in the pin to free it.

Right: Fig. 5.8. Spare inner tube.

the tire to the desired pressure (if the pump does not have a built-in pressure gauge, check with the separate pressure gauge).

8. If the valve is of the Presta type, tighten the nut at the end, and reinstall the dust cap for either type of valve.

REPLACE INNER TUBE

The easiest and quickest way to "fix" a bike with a punctured tire is to replace the inner tube. However, since there's a limit to the number of inner tubes you're likely to take along, and for the sake of economy, I suggest you also learn how to actually repair a punctured tube, which will be described under *Puncture Repair*.

Before commencing, remove the wheel from the bike.

TOOLS & EQUIPMENT:

• set of tire levers (preferably 3 thin flat ones)

• tire pump for the type of valve installed on the bike

- pressure gauge for the same type of valve

- spare tube of the same type and size as is installed on the bike

- preferably some talcum powder to treat the new tube so it does not deteriorate or adhere to the inside of the tire cover

- sometimes a pair of tweezers to remove sharp embedded objects from the tire cover

REMOVAL PROCEDURE:

1. Remove the dust cap from the valve and let any remaining air out of the tire by pushing in the pin in the valve (after unscrewing the little round nut in the case of a Presta valve).

2. If there is a nut screwed onto the base of the valve, remove it.

3. Push the valve into the tire as far as possible to create more space for the tire bead toward the center of the rim.

4. Manipulate the tire sidewall by hand, working all around to push the bead toward the deeper center section of the rim. Then work one area of the side from which you're working, some distance away from the valve, back up to the edge of the rim.

5. Place the end of the long part of the L-shaped tire lever under the tire bead over the top of the side of the rim, with the short end of the tire lever facing toward the center of the wheel. Then use it as a lever to push the bead of the tire up and over the side of the rim, hooking the notch in the short end of the lever onto a spoke.

6. Do the same with the second tire lever, 2–4 spokes further to one side.

7. If necessary (i.e. if the tire sidewall can't be pushed off the rim by hand at this point), do the same with the third tire lever.

8. At this stage, you can remove the first tire lever you installed (and, if necessary, you can use it as a fourth lever).

9. Remove the entire side of the tire cover off the rim by hand, working around gradually from the area where you used the tire levers.

10. Pull most of the inner tube out from between the tire cover and the rim.

11. Push the valve through the valve hole and remove the entire inner tube.

12. Check the condition of the tire cover inside and out, and remove any sharp embedded objects that may have been

Above: Fig. 5.11. Lifting the tire off the rim by hand.

Left: Fig. 5.9. Inserting first tire lever.

Right: Fig. 5.10. Two tire levers inserted.

the cause of the puncture (using tweezers if you can't get them out by hand).

INSTALLATION PROCEDURE

1. Check the condition of the rim tape that covers the deepest section of the rim bed to make sure it is intact and has the right width (it must just cover the deepest portion of the rim but not go up the sides) and no spoke ends are poking through (replace the rim tape and/or file off protruding spoke ends if necessary).

2. Install the new tube starting at the valve, carefully making sure it is embedded properly in the deepest section of the rim under the tire.

3. Inflate the tube just a little, so it is no longer "limp" but does not have noticeable pressure either.

4. Starting at the valve, pull the tire cover back over the rim, working it into the deepest section of the rim as you work your way around in both directions until it is in place over its entire circumference. The last part will probably be tough, but don't use a tire lever or any other tool to do this. Instead, achieve enough slack by working the bead deeper into the center section and pulling the entire tire toward the valve (you may have to let more air out of the tube). Then pull the last section over from the opposite side as shown in Fig. 5.14

5. Inflate the inner tube slightly and then "knead" the sidewalls until you're sure no part of the inner tube is caught in between the rim and the tire bead.

6. Inflate to the final pressure, making sure the tire cover gets seated properly as you do so. It's seated properly if the ridge on the side is the same distance from the rim all around the circumference on both sides. If necessary, correct it by first letting some air out, then "kneading" the tire, working all around until it is seated properly, then re- inflate.

7. Check the pressure with the pressure gauge and correct it if necessary.

PUNCTURE REPAIR

If you don't have (any more) spare inner tubes with you, or once you get home, you can usually repair a damaged inner tube by patching it. Most of the work is the same as what was described for replacing the inner tube, so this description only covers the actual patching.

TOOLS & EQUIPMENT:

* tire patch kit (adhesive patches, sand paper or abra-

Above: Fig. 5.12. Removing the tube.

Left: Fig. 5.13. Pushing tube over the rim.

Right: Fig. 5.14. Pulling the tire over the rim.

sive scraper, rubber solution, and talcum powder)

PROCEDURE:

1. Check the entire surface of the tube, starting at any location you may have identified as the probable cause of the puncture on account of damage to the tire.

2. If you can't easily locate the leak, inflate the tube and pass it along your ear or your eye, to listen or feel where air escapes. If you don't find it this way, dip the inflated tube in a basin with water and watch for escaping air bubbles—that's where the (or at least one) hole is. Since there may be more holes, continue the search all around the tube.

    If you have dipped the tire, dry it before proceeding. Make sure you identify every leak, because there may be more than one. Mark the location(s) of any leak(s) by drawing a circle that's bigger than the patch you will be using around it.

3. Rough up the area with the abrasive from the tire patch kit and wipe it clean.

4. Apply a thin, even layer of rubber solution to the area to be patched, slightly bigger than the patch you have selected, and let it dry for about 1 minute in hot weather, 2–3 minutes in cold weather—until the surface of the rubber solution becomes dull.

5. Pull one end of the protective layer (usually aluminum foil) from the patch without touching the adhesive side of the patch, and apply the patch to the treated area of the tube, centered on the hole while pulling off the remainder of the protective layer.

Above: Fig. 5.16. Roughing up the surface.

Left: Fig. 5.15. Marking the hole location.

Top right: Fig. 5.18. Spreading out adhesive.

Bottom right: Fig. 5.19. Applying the patch.

Below: Fig. 5.17. Applying the adhesive.

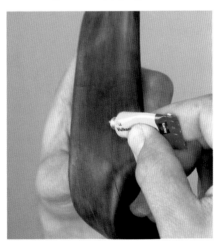

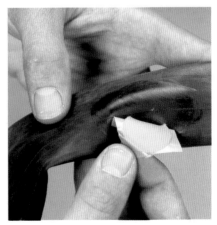

6. Apply firm pressure to the entire patch for about a minute, squeezing it by hand and rubbing it e.g. with the handle of a screwdriver while supporting the tire.

7. Check to make sure the patch has adhered properly over its entire surface (and redo Steps 3 through 6 if it has not).

8. Sprinkle some talcum powder over the patched area to prevent it from adhering to the inside of the tire cover. (Leaving the transparent plastic on the non-adhesive side of the patch has the same effect.)

9. Inflate the tube and wait about a minute to make sure it is not leaking, and if it is, repeat the repair for the same or any other hole you find.

10. Let the air out again and reinstall the tube under the tire cover over the rim as outlined in *Installation procedure*.

NOTE:

Make sure the rim tape is installed properly in the middle of the rim, covering the spoke nipples, and replace it if it is damaged or missing.

TIRE COVER REPAIR

Occasionally, you may be able to patch a tire cover if it has a small cut in it. However, it will be better to replace the tire completely if you can. If you do choose to patch it, follow the instructions above for tube repair and patch the inside cover with a small section cut from an old, thin tire. You'll have to use rubber adhesive on both the inside of the tire and on the patch. Sprinkle some talcum powder over the patch to prevent adhesion of the tire cover to the tube.

REPLACE TIRE COVER

When a tire cover is worn or damaged, it too has to be replaced. Make sure it has the right size, corresponding to the rim size. For mountain bike use, some tires are marked with a direction of rotation and sometimes there are different tires recommended for front and rear use. Pay attention to those details and make sure

Left Fig. 5.20. This is how a properly adhered patch should look.

Right: Fig. 5.21. Placing rim tape on the rim at the valve hole.

you get the right type and install it the right way round. (To get the right direction of rotation, visualize the tire on the bike, with the chain on the right—the top of the tire will rotate forward as you look down on it.) The description is based on the wheel being removed from the bike.

TOOLS & EQUIPMENT:

• set of 3 tire levers

• pump

• pressure gauge

• talcum powder

PROCEDURE:

1. Treat the inside of the new tire cover with talcum powder to prevent it adhering to the inner tube.

2. Deflate the inner tube and remove the tire cover and the inner tube as described in *Removal procedure* under *Inner Tube Replacement*.

3. Put one side of the new tire cover over the side of the rim

and push it into the center, making sure it faces the right way round if it's marked for a direction of location.

4. Put the inner tube back under the tire cover and then mount the other side of the tire cover over the rim, followed by a check and tube inflation in accordance with the *Installation procedure* under *Inner Tube Replacement*.

TUBULAR TIRES

If your bike has tubular tires, or sew-ups, you will at least have to learn how to replace them in case they go flat on a ride. Fortunately, tubular tires are much less susceptible to so-called "snake-bites" than wired-on tires. That's due to the fact that almost all of the tire diameter is outside the rim, whereas a good part of a regular wired-on tire is inside the rim.

Tubular tires are mounted on different rims, so-called Sprint rims, which have a cross-section as illustrated in the right-most detail of Fig. 7.4 in Chapter 7, to which they are glued with special adhesive or with double-sided ad-

hesive tape. I much prefer the latter method, which is much easier to use than adhesive. If the tire is mounted on carbon-fiber rims (e.g as used with disk wheels and their bladed variants), make sure the tire is mounted with an adhesive that is compatible with carbon fiber, since the adhesive used with metal rims does not hold adequately on carbon fiber rims.

Since patching a tubular tire is rather tricky, it's not the kind of thing you'll want to do by the side of the road but at home with plenty of time on your hands, Consequently, when riding a bike with tubular tires, you should never leave home without a spare.

Keep spare tubular tires (regardless whether new or repaired) slightly inflated in a cool, dry place.

REPLACE TUBULAR TIRE

TOOLS & EQUIPMENT:

- spare tubular tire

- adhesive or adhesive tape

- acetone or waterless hand cleaner

- cleaning cloth

- water

- tire pump with Presta head

REMOVAL PROCEDURE:

1. Make sure the tire is completely deflated (let any remaining air out if needed).

2. If there is a round nut on the valve holding it in at the rim, remove that nut.

3. Starting opposite the valve, roll the tire off sideways as shown in the illustration, working around in both directions until it can be removed at the valve.

4. Clean any adhesive remnants off the rim with acetone or waterless hand cleaner.

5. Spread a thin, even layer of adhesive on the tire seat bed area of the rim.

   • In case tape will be used, peal off the end of the backing

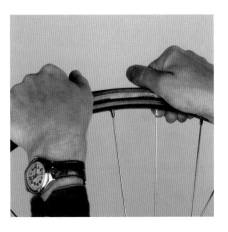

Left: Fig. 5.22. Inspecting inside the tire cover.

Right: Fig. 5.23. Rolling a tubular tire off the rim.

strip from one side; start placing the tape next to the valve hole working all around, peeling off the protective strip finishing by overlapping the valve hole. Cut a hole in the tape at the valve hole. Firmly push the tape down all around (using e.g. the end of a screwdriver handle). Then remove the top backing strip.

6. Put a 2-inch wide strip of paper across the adhesive just opposite the valve hole. This will make it easier to start removal of the tire the next time it has to be replaced.

7. Wet your fingers with water and slightly dampen the adhesive (or adhesive tape) all around. This gives you more time to position the tire accurately.

8. Stretch a new tire by holding one part with your foot and pulling up the opposite section with both hands (don't do this if it's a previously used tire).

9. Slightly inflate the tire, just enough to make it limp.

10. Insert the valve through the valve hole of the rim and continue placing the tire all around, making sure it is centered.

11. Inflate the tire to its final pressure.

12. Tear off the projecting ends of the paper strip opposite the valve hole.

TUBULAR TIRE REPAIR

Once the tire has been removed from the rim, you can usually salvage it by patching it, though it's quite time consuming.

TOOLS & EQUIPMENT:

*   tubular patch kit

*   sharp, pointed knife

*   pen or pencil

*   pump with Presta head

PROCEDURE:

1. Inflate the tire and listen for escaping air to locate the hole. If necessary, dip in water and watch for escaping air bubbles. Then mark the location and deflate the tire fur-

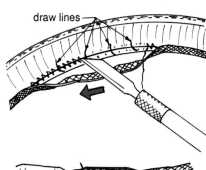

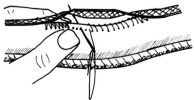

Fig. 5.24. Tubular tire repair.

ther if the leak is so slow that it is still under pressure.

2. Using a thin flat object, like a screwdriver, remove the backing tape from the tire over about 8 inches (20 cm) in the area of the hole.

3. Draw a line every half inch or so (15 mm) perpendicularly across the seam of the tire to aid in lining up the two sides when sewing it back up.

4. Carefully cut the stitching and remove the loose ends.

5. Push the inside backing strip out of the way and pull the tube out of the casing, then repair the tube as described for a regular wired-on tire starting on page 46.

6. Insert the tube and pull the internal backing strip over it.

7. Pushing back the tube to prevent damage, carefully sew the seam back together. Keep the stitching slack enough to allow flattening out the seam later. Work the ends of the twine back under the stitching to prevent unraveling.

8. Using tire solution on both the tire cover and the backing tape, glue the tape back on.

6 HUB MAINTENANCE

The hub is the center of any wheel. While the subject of holding the wheel in the bike was already covered in Chapter 4, this chapter deals with the hub itself.

PARTS OF THE HUB

The hub consists of an axle, a set of ball bearings, and the hub shell. On the sides, the hub shell has flanges to accommodate the holes through which the spokes are inserted. Quick-release hubs have hollow axles, while they are solid for "bolted-on" hubs, which are held on by axle nuts.

The hub shell is usually made of aluminum alloy, although it may be steel on a low-end bike, or carbon fiber at the high end. The number of spoke holes in the flanges must correspond to the number of spokes in the wheel, each flange usually (but, on a rear wheel, not always) holding half the total number of spokes.

HUB BEARINGS

The hub's ball bearings may be either adjustable cup-and-cone bearings or "sealed" cartridge bearings.

Above: Fig. 6.2. Close-up of front wheel hub.

Fig. 6.1. Cross-section of conventional (adjustable) hub.

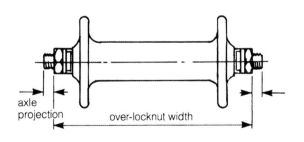

Fig. 6.3. Hub dimensioning.

Hub maintenance consists of adjusting, lubricating, overhauling, or replacing the bearings, although in rare cases the axle may have to be replaced as well. This work can be done with the wheel left assembled, whereas replacing the hub requires rebuilding the entire wheel.

HUB BEARING CHECK

Do this work in conjunction with the annual overhaul—and whenever you detect symptoms of wear, such as high resistance or looseness of the wheel.

TOOLS & EQUIPMENT:

- Usually none required.

PROCEDURE:

1. Make sure the wheel is firmly held in the frame or the fork.

2. Check whether the wheel turns freely by lifting the wheel off the ground and spinning it slowly by hand. It should come to rest with the valve at the bottom. If not, the bearings must be adjusted or replaced.

3. Check whether there is play in the bearings, i.e. whether they are too loose, by holding the bike at the front fork (for the front wheel) or the frame (for the rear wheel) and trying to move the rim sideways relative to this point. If it can be moved loosely, the bearings are too loose and must be adjusted or replaced.

HUB BEARING ADJUSTMENT

This procedure only applies to hubs with cup-and-cone bearings. If the hub has cartridge bearings, refer to the instructions *Cartridge Bearing Maintenance* on page 54.

TOOLS & EQUIPMENT:

- cone wrenches

- open-ended wrenches or combination wrenches

PROCEDURE:

1. Remove the wheel from the bike.

2. While holding the cone firmly on one side with a cone wrench, loosen the locknut on the same side by about one full turn, using either another cone wrench or a regular wrench.

3. Lift the keyed washer that's installed between the cone and the nut so it comes loose from the cone.

- If the bearing was too loose, tighten the cone about $1/8$ turn at a time while holding the locknut on the opposite side steady with a wrench.

- If the bearing was too tight, loosen the cone about $1/8$ turn at a time while holding the cone on the opposite side steady with another cone wrench.

4. Tighten the locknut while holding the cone on the same side, then check the adjustment, and if needed repeat the procedure until the hub runs smoothly. If you can't get it to run smoothly, overhaul the hub.

5. Reinstall the wheel in the bike.

Above: Fig. 6.5. Manufacturer's drawing of front hub.

Left: Fig. 6.4. Rear cassette-type hub.

Right: Fig. 6.6. Lifting protective seal off hub bearing.

LUBRICATION & OVERHAULING ADJUSTABLE BEARINGS HUB

This is best done in conjunction with the annual inspection, or whenever a bearing problem can't be solved with adjustment as described above. On a rear wheel, start on the left side of the wheel, because the bearing on the chain side is usually not easily accessible.

TOOLS & EQUIPMENT:

- cone wrenches
- open-ended or combination wrenches
- thin, flat object with leverage, e.g. a wide screwdriver
- cleaning cloths
- solvent
- bearing grease

DISMANTLING PROCEDURE:

1. Remove the wheel from the bike and remove the quick-release or the axle nuts and washers.

2. Holding the cone on one side with one cone wrench, remove the locknut on the same side with another cone wrench or a regular wrench.

3. Lift off and remove the lock washer, noting that it has an internal tag, or "key," that fits in a groove that runs lengthwise in the axle. Also remove any other spacers and washers that may be installed between the cone and the locknut.

4. Place the wheel horizontally with a cloth under the hub. Loosen and remove the cone, holding the cone on the opposite side with a cone wrench. Catch all the bearing balls in the cloth.

5. Pull the axle out of the hub, with the cone and the locknut still installed on the opposite side, again carefully catching the bearing balls in the cloth.

OVERHAULING, LUBRICATING, & REASSEMBLY PROCEDURE:

1. Carefully pry off any plastic or Neoprene dust caps at the hub ends, using a thin flat tool (but preferably leave them in place if they are made of metal).

2. Thoroughly clean all parts—bearing balls, cones,

Left: Fig. 6.7. Tightening lock nut and cone relative to each other.

Right: Fig. 6.8. Cone removed from adjustable bearing.

axle, bearing races, and dust caps.

3. Inspect all parts, especially the contact surfaces of bearing races, cones, and bearing balls. Replace any parts that show signs of roughness, grooves, pitting, or corrosion.

4. Check the axle to make sure it is still straight by rolling it over a smooth level surface (e.g. a table top)—replace it if it wobbles.

5. Fill the bearing cups with grease and push the bearing balls in (if you're in doubt about the correct number of balls, it should be one less than the maximum you could squeeze in). Then reinstall the dust caps, if they had been removed.

6. Reinsert the axle from the same side as from which it was removed, guiding it carefully so the end does not push any bearing balls out of the bearing cups.

7. Holding the end of the axle to which the cone and locknut are still attached, install the other bearing cone until almost tight—there should be just a little play left in the bearings.

8. Place the keyed washer on the axle, aligning the tab with the groove in the axle. Also install any other spacers and washers that may have been present between the cone and the locknut.

9. Install the locknut and tighten it firmly against the underlying cone.

10. Check to make sure the bearings are now adjusted to provide smooth rotation without play, and if not, readjust them.

11. Reinstall the wheel.

NOTE:

If cup-and-cone bearings can no longer be adjusted to run smoothly, the cones can be replaced, and if even that does not do the trick, the bearing cups

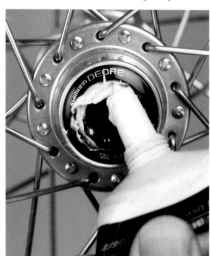

may have to be replaced. Since that operation requires special tools, it's best left to a bike shop mechanic.

CARTRIDGE BEARING MAINTENANCE

The "sealed" cartridge bearings used on most modern bikes require less maintenance because they are better protected against the intrusion of dirt, and the lubricant is better retained inside the bearings.

To replenish the lubricant, which should be done once a year, proceed as follows:

TOOLS & EQUIPMENT:

• thin screwdriver for raising the seal

• squeeze bottle or can with SAE 60 mineral oil

• cloth

• tire lever or similar flat object for pushing the seal in

PROCEDURE:

1. Remove the wheel from the bike and place it horizontally on the work bench.

2. Lift the neoprene seal that covers the accessible bearings up with the screwdriver.

Left: Fig. 6.9. Lubricating adjustable (cup-and-cone) bearing.

Right: Fig. 6.10. Adjusting bearings on hub with cup-and-cone bearing.

3. While holding up the seal with the screwdriver, squirt some mineral oil past it into the bearing until it runs out the other side, catching all excess oil with the cloth, and wiping all parts clean afterward.

4. Remove the screwdriver and push the seal back into place by hand or with the aid of a flat object, such as a tire lever.

5. To gain access to the hidden bearing inside the cassette of the rear wheel (on the right, or chain side), the bearing on the left would have to be removed first, a job best left to a bike shop mechanic who has the right tools for that.

6. Reinstall the wheel.

CARTRIDGE BEARING REPLACEMENT NOTE:

If the bearings are loose or cannot be made to operate smoothly with lubrication, they will have to be replaced by a bike shop mechanic using special tools.

7
RIM & SPOKE MAINTENANCE

This chapter deals with the rim and the spokes, as well as the wheel as a complete structure. When the wheel gets damaged, it's likely to be the rim and the spokes that take the blow,

THE SPOKED WHEEL

Take a look at the way a bicycle wheel is built up. Although there are exceptions among lightweight and/or aerodynamic wheels, the

typical way a wheel is built up is as shown in Fig. 7.1.

There may be 24, 28, 32, or 36 spokes per wheel (or even more on tandem wheels). Every other one around the rim runs to the left-side hub flange, the other ones to the right-side hub flange. The spokes on each side of the wheel provide radial and lateral (i.e. sideways) rigidity by pulling

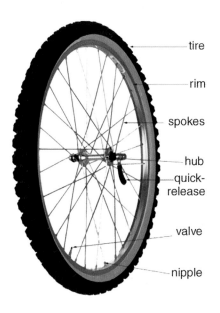

- tire
- rim
- spokes
- hub
- quick-release
- valve
- nipple

Fig. 7.1. Parts of the wheel.

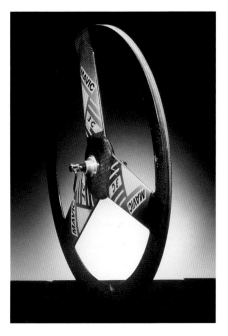

Above: Fig. 7.2. Carbon-fiber aerodynamic wheels like this are pretty strong, but they can't be repaired if they do get damaged.

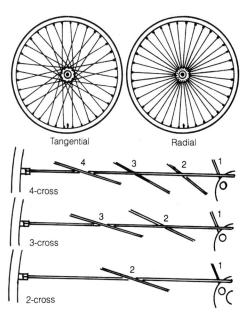

Tangential   Radial

4-cross

3-cross

2-cross

Fig. 7.3. Spoking pattern overview.

the rim from both sides. To-gether, they balance the wheel both radially and laterally.

The spokes on each side of the wheel form a particular pattern (which is usually, though not always, the same on both sides). If they all run radially straight from the rim to the hub flange, it's called radial spoking. If each spoke crosses one other spoke on the same side, it's called 1-cross spoking; if it crosses two other spokes on the same side, it's called 2-cross spoking, etc.

Before you start work on a wheel, check the number of spokes and the spoking pattern, and if you replace any or all spokes, adhere to the same pattern. You will also need spokes of the same length (which is not necessarily the same on both sides) and thickness (referred to as "gauge").

Another thing to check before you start work on the wheel is the spoke tension of a similar well-built new wheel at a bike shop. Do that by squeezing a pair of neighboring spokes together and noticing the resistance. Then "pluck" them like musical strings and note the pitch—higher tension results in a higher pitch. When maintaining or rebuilding a wheel, aim for the same spoke tension.

SPECIAL WHEELS

Some aerodynamic wheels don't use conventional wire spokes. They're often made of carbon fiber, or they may use special spokes and a special hub. They are hardly subject to mainte-nance—if bent or broken, the entire wheel usually has to be replaced or repaired at a bike shop.

THE RIM

Most rims are of one of the patterns shown in Fig. 7.4, although their depth and width may vary greatly. The inward-facing bulges at the tip of the sides serve to hook the bead of the tire into place.

The rim diameter must match the tire size—typically mountain bikes have 559 mm diameter rims and road bikes have 622 mm diameter rims. The width may vary from quite narrow (like 14 mm) for the lightest road racing bikes to very wide (like 32 mm) for some mountain bikes.

The number of spoke holes must match the number of spokes in the wheel. Finally, the valve hole must be the right size—6.5 mm for a Presta valve

or 9 mm for a Schrader valve (or 7.5 mm for a Woods valve).

WHEEL TRUING CHECK

Wheel damage is usually causes by a blow to the rim, deforming it either radially or laterally. Deformed this way, it's called "out of true," and the trick is to get it trued again. As a result of the deformation, some of the spokes become looser and others tighter. Another reason the wheel may be out of true can be due to loosening of the spokes in the nipples.

Often, though not always, the damage can be repaired by selective re-tensioning of the spokes. Here's how you can check the extent of the damage.

TOOLS & EQUIPMENT:

* Usually none required, although a wheel truing stand, preferably with built-in gauges, makes the job easier.

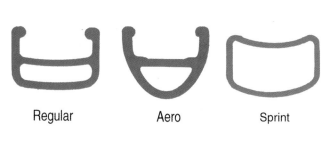

Regular   Aero   Sprint

Fig. 7.4. Rim types (Sprint rims are for tubular tires).

Right: Fig. 7.5. Wheel truing check without use of truing stand.

PROCEDURE:

1. Place the bike in the work stand or turn it upside-down (protecting any items mounted on the handlebars). If you have a wheel truing stand, remove the wheel and mount it in the truing stand.

2. Slowly spin the wheel by hand and observe the distance between both sides of the rim and the frame or the truing stand. Observe as it rotates whether the wheel wobbles sideways, in which case it's laterally out of true, or up-and-down, in which case it's radially out of true. Also check whether any of the spokes are broken.

3. If there appears to be a gradual deformation over a significant area, you will probably be able to fix it by either radial or lateral truing, described below under *Wheel Truing*.

4. If there is a short, sudden deformation of the side of the rim, that is probably due to direct-impact damage of the rim, which cannot be repaired satisfactorily, and calls for replacement of the rim.

5. If inspection of the wheel reveals that one or more of the spokes are broken, they must be replaced, after which the wheel has to be trued as well.

WHEEL TRUING

If the wheel truing check has established that it is out of true, this work will bring it back into shape.

TOOLS & EQUIPMENT:

- spoke wrench

- if possible, truing stand, although it can be done using the bike's frame or front fork instead

- adhesive tape or chalk for marking

- sometimes penetrating oil and a cloth

LATERAL TRUING PROCEDURE:

1. On the basis of the wheel truing check described above, mark (e.g. with pieces of adhesive tape wrapped around the nearest spokes or chalk marks on the tire) which section of the wheel is too far to

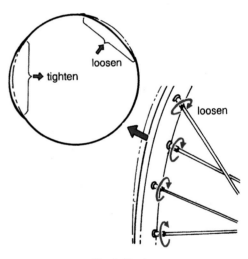

Radial truing

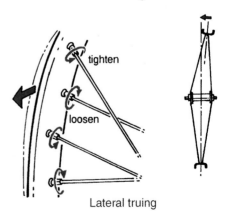

Lateral truing

Fig. 7.8. Wheel truing procedure.

Left: Fig. 7.6 Nipple heads as seen from inside the rim.

Above: Fig. 7.7. Tightening or loosening spokes.

the left or the right relative to the center.

2. In the area thus marked, loosen the spokes that lead to the same side as to which the buckle deviates from the center, and tighten the spokes that run to the other side. Do this by turning the nipples with the spoke wrench— about one turn at the highest point of the buckle and gradually less to ¼ turn at the end of the buckled portion.

• Looking from the center of the wheel toward the rim, loosening is achieved when you turn clockwise, and tightening when you turn counterclockwise.

• If the spokes are corroded solidly in the nipples, so the nipples won't turn properly, spray some penetrating oil at the points where the spokes disappear into the nipples, then wait 2–3 minutes before trying again.

3. Repeat Step 2 (but turning the nipples less and less as you get closer to the desired effect) until the sideways wobble is eliminated.

RADIAL TRUING PROCEDURE:

Using the same technique as described in Step 1 of the preceding *Lateral truing procedure*, identify the "flat spot" or the "high spot" of the rim by marking the nearest spokes. Then loosen the spokes in the "flat" area and tighten the ones in the "high" area until the up-and-down wobble, or "hop," is eliminated.

EMERGENCY REPAIR OF BUCKLED WHEEL

If the damage occurs suddenly during a ride in the form of a badly buckled ("pretzeled") wheel, e.g. as a result of hitting an obstacle, you may be able to make a provisional repair on the spot. Ride very carefully after this, because the wheel may suddenly collapse on you if you ride too fast in corners. Once you get home, do a thorough inspection and repair, which may well mean rebuilding or replacing the entire wheel.

TOOLS & EQUIPMENT:

• spoke wrench

Left: Fig. 7.9. Special wheel with straight-pull spokes.

Right: Fig. 7.10. Emergency repair o af buckled wheel.

PROCEDURE:

1. Remove the wheel from the bike.

2. Find a suitable step, such as a curb stone, on which you can support one part of the rim while the other part is supported at a lower point and the hub axle stays clear of the road surface. Place the wheel in such a way that the most severe part of the outward deformation faces down on the higher support point.

3. Carefully but forcefully push down on the sections of the rim that are 60 degrees offset either side of the buckled portion. Continue or repeat until the rim is reasonably straight.

4. Place the wheel back in the bike and do a truing check as described above, then adjust the spoke tension as well as possible under the circumstances until the wobble is minimized.

THE SPOKES

Spokes are measured in mm as shown in Fig. 7.11, i.e. from the inside of the bend to the tip of the screw-threaded end. They are available in a wide array of sizes for different combinations of hub, rim, and spoking pattern. Their thickness is also measured in mm, while the nipples must be matched with the spoke thickness and screw thread.

Most spokes are made of stainless steel. Often spokes have different thicknesses in different sections. This is referred to as "butted," meaning that the ends (butts) are thicker than the middle section—a little lighter and more flexible, reducing the risk of breakage.

REPLACE INDIVIDUAL SPOKE

This is necessary if one or more of the spokes are broken, usually at the bent portion near the head of the spoke, where it is attached to the hub flange. Replace broken spokes as soon as possible, because if you ride with one broken spoke, there is a great likelihood of additional wheel damage and more spokes breaking. Do this

work with the wheel removed from the bike.

NOTE:

On some rims, the spoke holes are not reinforced with ferrules, in which case there may be a little washer between the rim and the head of the nipple. When replacing spokes and nipples on a rim like that, don't forget to reinstall the washers.

TOOLS & EQUIPMENT:

- spoke wrench
- cloth and a speck of lubricant
- sometimes tire levers and a pump

PROCEDURE:

1. Remove the remaining pieces of the broken spoke, unscrewing the outside portion from the nipple. If it won't unscrew, remove the tire and pull nipple and the remaining piece of the spoke out through the rim.

   • If the spoke seems very loose in the nipple, you should also replace the nipple. Do that by removing a section of

the tire and the tube as described in Chapter 5, lifting the rim tape, and prying out the old nipple. Then insert the new one and reinstall the rim tape, the tube, and the tire.

2. Buy a spoke that's exactly the same length and thickness as the other spokes on the same side of the wheel.

3. Check how the spoke that runs to the second hub flange hole from the spoke to be replaced runs—whether the head is on the inside or the outside of the hub flange and whether it goes over or under the crossing spokes.

4. Apply a little lubricant to the threaded end of the spoke and then route it the same way as the one you observed in Step 3, screwing the nipple onto the screw-threaded end of the spoke until it has the

Above: Fig. 7.12. Threading a spoke through spoke hole in the hub flange.

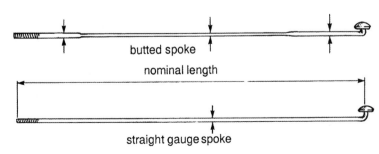

nipple

butted spoke

nominal length

straight gauge spoke

Fig. 7.11. Spoke details.

same tension as other spokes on the same side of the wheel.

5. Check the wheel as described under *Wheel Truing Check* and make any truing corrections as may be necessary following the *Wheel Truing* procedure.

EMERGENCY SPOKE

To be able to handle spoke breakage while riding, you can make an emergency spoke that can be inserted easily without removing the cogs or the freewheel. Buy a spoke of the same gauge but about ½ in. (12 mm) longer than a regular spoke for your wheel, and bend it as shown in Fig. 7.13.

When a spoke breaks while riding, unscrew it from the nipple and discard it. Now insert the hooked end at the rim and screw the other end into the nipple until taut. Do replace it with a "real" spoke once you get back home, though.

REPLACE RIM

Normally, rebuilding a wheel is a rather involved job that takes lots of practice to do effectively (or lots of time until you have lots of practice). However, often it's pos-

sible to follow a simple procedure of unhooking the spokes on one rim and installing them into the new rim as you go along. The wheel must be removed from the bike, and the tire and tube from the rim.

This method only works if you are replacing the rim by an identical rim. If you have to replace the spokes or the hub as well, instructions for wheel building can be found in Chapter 8. (Alternately, you can leave this job to a bike shop mechanic.)

TOOLS & EQUIPMENT:

*   spoke wrench

*   if possible, truing stand, although it can be done using the bike's frame or front fork instead

*   adhesive tape

*   lubricant and cloth

*   sometimes penetrating oil

PROCEDURE:

1. Place the new rim on top of the old one and align the valve hole of the new rim with that of the existing one, to make sure the two rims are indeed identical in size, depth, and hole pattern.

2. Tape the two rims together in two or three spots around the circumference.

3. Starting at a spoke next to the valve hole and working around the wheel, undo one spoke at a time by unscrewing the nipple, lubricating the screw-threaded end of the spoke, installing the nipple in the corresponding spoke hole on the new rim, and screwing the nipple onto the spoke, leaving about 3 mm (⅛ in.) of the spoke screw thread exposed.

    *   If the nipples are too stiff on the spokes of the old rim, apply some penetrating oil to all the spoke ends at the nipples first and wait 2–3 minutes before trying to unscrew them.

4. When all the spokes are attached to the new rim, re-

bend as shown   Detail

Fig. 7.13. Home-made emergency spoke.

Above: Fig. 7.14. Replacing identical rim.

move the old rim, then gradually tighten the spokes with the wheel in a truing stand or in the bike.

5. Grab the spokes in groups of 4, two neighboring crossing spokes on each side, and squeeze them together force-fully. This operation is referred to as "stress relieving."

6. Check the wheel for lateral and radial true, and make any adjustments necessary.

7. Check inside the rim, and file off any spoke ends that may project from the nipples.

8. Install the new rim tape, the tire and the tube. Inflate the tire and re-true the wheel if necessary.

10. Check and re-tension and true the wheel after about 50 km (30 miles) of riding.

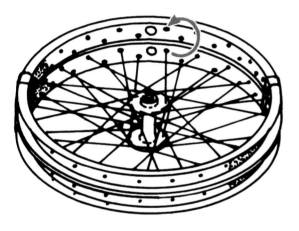

Fig. 7.15. Transferring spokes to new rim.

Top right: Fig. 7.16. Stress-relieving sets of spokes.

Bottom right: Fig. 7.17. Special radially spoked wheel with straight-pull spokes (i.e. spokes without a bend at the head).

8
WHEEL BUILDING

Rebuilding a wheel is not a job for everyone: a professional can do it much faster than any home mechanic. On the other hand, it's wonderful therapy, gives great satisfaction, and becomes easier as you do it more often.

Before you start, take a very close look at the old wheel (or another similar wheel) and the various descriptions and drawings in this chapter and the preceding one that show spoking details—try to

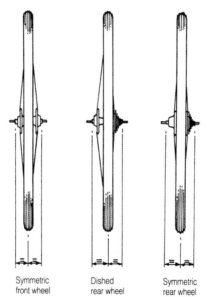

Symmetric
front wheel

Dished
rear wheel

Symmetric
rear wheel

Fig. 8.1. Symmetrical and dished wheels.

Left: Fig. 8.2. Overview of a newly built wheel.

Right: Fig. 8.3. Use of spoke length gauge to measure the length of a spoke.

understand what's going on before you start.

SPOKE LENGTH DETERMINATION

Make sure you get the right spoke length for the rim and hub in question. Ask at the bike shop, telling them which hub and which rim you will be combining, which spoking pattern (radial, one-, two-, three-, or four-cross), and how many spokes will be used.

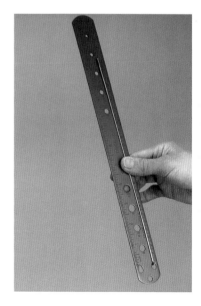

Most modern wheels are built with 32 or 28 spokes, whereas 36 spokes are common on utility bikes, and tandem wheels may have even more spokes. On an off-set, or "dished," rear wheel, the spokes on the right side should be about 3 mm ($^1/_8$ in.) shorter than those on the left side; or, if you can't find the optimum spoke size, deviate a little on the low side for the spokes on the right side, a little on the high side for the left-side spokes.

If you have a programmable calculator, you can use the following formula to calculate the spoke length yourself (all dimensions in mm).

$$L = \sqrt{(A^2 + B^2 + C^2)} - .5\,S$$

where:

L = spoke length

A = r sin (T)

B = R — r cos (T)

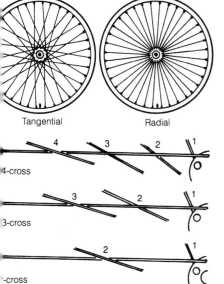

Fig. 8.4. Spoking patterns overview.

C = offset from outside hub flange to center of wheel (measured as shown in Detail A of Fig. 8.5); on a front wheel, it is ½ the total hub width; on a rear wheel it will be different on both sides

r = ½ the effective hub diameter (measured as shown in detail B)

R = ½ the effective rim diameter (measured as shown in detail C)

T = 360 X / N

X = number of spoke crossings desired

N = number of spokes per hub flange (usually, one half total number of spokes)

S = spoke hole diameter in hub flange

SPOKE LENGTH CHECK

If you're scared off by the formula, here's a method of determining relatively painlessly whether you are using the correct spoke length. It is based on the principle that any plane is determined by three points. Use this method whenever you are not absolutely sure whether you have the correct spoke length.

TOOLS & EQUIPMENT:

- spoke wrench
- medium screwdriver
- lubricant and cloth

PROCEDURE:

1. Take six spokes and nipples; lubricate the spoke ends and wipe off the excess.

2. Hold the hub upright in front of you. On the upper hub flange, select three holes that are equally spaced (every sixth in the case of a 36-hole hub,

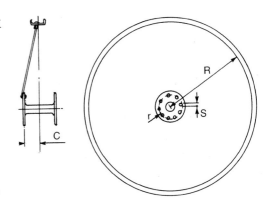

Fig. 8.5. Spoke-size-calculation basis.

Table 8.1. Spoke hole spacing in hub for neighboring spokes in rim.

No. of spokes in wheel	1-cross angle	spaces	2-cross angle	spaces	3-cross angle	spaces	4-cross angle	spaces	5-cross angle	spaces
24	75°	2½	135°	4½	–	–	–	–	–	–
28	64.3°	2½	115.7°	4½	167.1°	6½	–	–	–	–
32	56.3°	2½	101.3°	4½	146.3°	6½	–	–	–	–
36	50°	2½	90°	4½	130°	6½	170°	8½	–	–
40	45°	2½	81°	4½	117°	6½	153°	8½	–	–
44	40.9°	2½	73.6°	4½	106.4°	6½	139.1°	8½	171.8°	10½
48	37.5°	2½	67.5°	4½	97.5°	6½	127.5°	8½	157.5°	10½

which has 18 holes per flange. If the hub has more or less than 36 holes, you may not be able to space completely equally. Just make sure the spokes are spaced as evenly as possible, with an odd number of empty spoke holes in the flange between the spokes).

If the hub has holes that are alternately countersunk ("beveled"), select holes that are beveled on the inside. Put a spoke through each of these holes from the outside through to the inside.

3. Inspect the spoke holes in the rim. Take the hole next to the valve hole that is off-set up (on most rims sold in the U.S., that is the first hole going counterclockwise, but it may also be the first one going clockwise). Attach one of the three spokes with the nipple in this hole. Mark it with adhesive tape—we'll call it "Spoke 1."

4. Count out the same number of holes that are offset upward as there are vacant holes in the hub, going the same direction (clockwise or counterclockwise). Place the other two spokes in the corresponding holes determined this way. Now the spokes in the upper hub flange should be connected to similarly spaced holes that are off-set upward in the rim—correct if necessary.

5. Turn the wheel over, so that the side without spokes faces up.

6. Visually line up the two hub flanges, noting how the holes in the near flange are positioned between the holes in the far flange. I'll call this off-set from one hole in the one flange to the nearest hole in the other flange a "half space," while I'll call the space between consecutive holes in the same flange a "whole space."

7. To find the location for the first spoke inserted on the flange that is on top now, read off the number of spaces from the table, as a function of the number of spokes and the number of spoke crossings required (e.g. 6½ for a four-cross pattern with 32 spokes).

Count the appropriate number of spaces from the hole where Spoke 1 (marked with tape) is located in the direction of the valve hole (i.e. going counterclockwise if the valve hole is counterclockwise from the spoke). In the hub flange hole thus established,

insert a spoke from the outside to the inside, and attach this spoke to the free spoke hole in the rim immediately adjacent to the valve hole.

8. Count the same number of spoke holes in the hub on either side of this spoke as you count between corresponding spokes on the lower flange on either side of Spoke 1, inserting the two remaining spokes there, again from the outside to the inside.

9. Attach these spokes to the rim in the holes that are in the same relative position to each other as the two spokes on either side of the valve hole.

10. Check whether you've got something that looks like Fig. 8.6, and if not, where you went wrong. Correct if necessary.

11. Tighten the six spokes gradually until the wheel is reasonably tight and centered (front wheel) or appropriately off-set ("dished" rear wheel) as required. If significant thread is exposed under the nipple (more than 1 thread), choose a longer spoke; if any part of the spoke protrudes beyond the nipple inside the rim, choose a shorter spoke—and start all over again. If the spoke length is correct, continue building the wheel more or less as described in the following spoking procedure, starting at step 4.

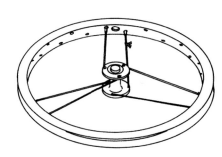

Fig. 8.6. Six-spoke length check.

NOTE:

If you are building a radially spoked (front) wheel, insert all spokes from the inside to the outside, so they all lie on the outside of the hub flanges.

SPOKING THE WHEEL

This instruction is based on the assumption that you have determined the correct spoke length. If you're not sure, first carry out the check described above under *Spoke Length Check*, after which you'll be well on your way and can pick up the instructions starting at step 4. If you re rebuilding a wheel using an old hub or an old rim (or both), first cut away all the old spokes and remove them. If you're reusing the spokes and the hub, follow the procedure *Replace Rim* in Chapter 7.

TOOLS & EQUIPMENT:

* spoke wrench
* medium size screwdriver
* lubricant and cloth

SPOKING PROCEDURE:

1. Lubricate the threaded ends and wipe off excess lubricant.

2. Take 8 spokes (assuming a 32-spoke wheel—more or less for other wheels), and put one through every second hole in one of the hub flanges from the outside to the inside. If holes are alternately countersunk on the inside and the outside of the hub flange, select those holes that are countersunk on the inside.

3. Putting the hub in front of you, held vertically with the batch of spokes stuck through the upper flange. Find the spoke hole in the hub that's immediately next to the valve hole and is off-set upward. Take one spoke and attach it with the nipple to that hole; mark this spoke (e.g. with tape). I'll refer to it as "Spoke 1." Screw on the nipple about five turns.

4. Similarly attach the other spokes so far installed in the hub into every fourth hole in the rim. If you followed the procedure *Spoke Length Check*, you already have three

of them—just put in the remaining spokes.

5. Check to make sure all these spokes are attached to spoke holes that are offset upward in the rim, and that three free spoke holes remain between each pair of consecutive spokes in the rim, one free hole in the hub.

6. Turn the wheel over and establish whether the remaining free hole immediately next to the valve hole is oriented clockwise or counterclockwise. Select the spoke holes in the flange now nearest to you that are each off-set half a space from the spokes already installed on the far flange in that same direction. Insert the next set of 8 (or whatever is the appropriate number) spokes in these

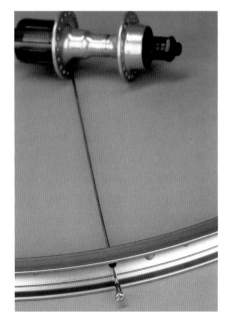

Above: Fig. 8.8. The first spoke installed in hub flange and rim.

Left: Fig. 8.7. Wheel building parts and tools: Rim, hub, spokes, nipples, length gauge, spoke wrench, and nipple driver.

holes, leaving a free hole between each set of consecutive spokes.

7. Locate Spoke 1, and count out the appropriate number of spaces to determine where the next spoke is. Attach it in the free spoke hole on the other side of the valve hole, counting clockwise if the free spoke hole is also clockwise from the valve hole, counterclockwise if the free hole is counterclockwise from the valve hole. If you followed the *Spoke Length Check* procedure, this has already been determined —just install the missing spokes.

8. Attach the remaining spokes so far inserted in the hub into every fourth spoke hole in the rim.

9. You should now have sets of two spokes, each set separated by two free holes in the rim and by one free hole in the hub flanges. Make any corrections that may be required.

10. Insert the next batch of spokes from the inside to the outside in one of the hub flanges.

11. Take any one of these spokes and "lace" it to cross the ap-

propriate number of spokes on the same hub flange for the crossing pattern selected, always crossing under the last one. If you're building a 3-cross wheel, that will be over the first, over the second, and then forced under the third crossing spoke. Attach this spoke in the next free hole in the rim that's offset in the corresponding direction. If it doesn't fit, you either have the wrong spoke length for the pattern selected, have tightened the other spokes too much (rarely the case), or you made a mistake somewhere along the line—check and restart if necessary.

12. Do the same with the last batch of spokes, inserting them in the free holes in the other hub flange from the inside to the outside, making the right crossings; then in-

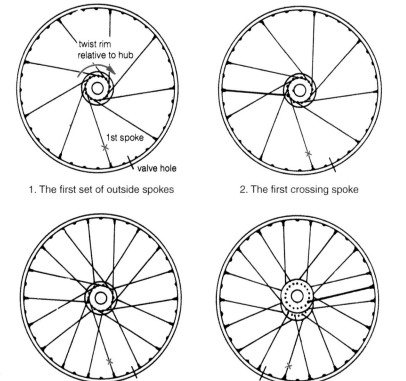

1. The first set of outside spokes

2. The first crossing spoke

3. All spokes on one side

4. The first spoke on the opposite side

Fig. 8.9. Wheel building sequence.

Above: Fig. 8.10. The first set of spokes installed, the second set ready to install.

stall them in the remaining spoke holes in the rim.

13. You now have a complete but loosely spoked wheel. Once more, check to make sure the pattern is correct as you intended, then start tightening the spoke nipples progressively, working around several times, first using the screwdriver, then—when the nipples begin to get tighter— with the spoke wrench. Don't tighten too much though: it should remain easy to turn the nipples with the spoke wrench.

14. Check whether the wheel is correctly centered between the locknuts at the wheel axle, as outlined in step 3 of the procedure *Wheel Truing* in Chapter 7, and the subsequent note.

15. Install the wheel in the truing stand (or the bike, which should be hung up off the ground by saddle and handlebars or placed upside-down). Now make the same kind of corrections as outlined under *Wheel Truing* in Chapter 7, until the wheel is perfectly round and has no lateral deflection.

16. Proceed to tighten the spokes equally all around. It's hard to explain in writing how tight is right. Just compare with another good wheel (ask in the bike shop) to develop a feel for the right tension. Tension is checked by means of a spoke tension gauge or simply by pushing spokes together in crossed pairs at a point between the rim and the last cross. On an off-set rear wheel, the right side spokes (i.e. those on the chain side) should be considerably tighter than those on the other side. All the spokes on the same side of a wheel must be equally tight.

17. Take spokes together in sets of four—two nearby sets of crossing spokes on each side of the wheel—and squeeze them together quite forcefully. This will bend the spokes into their final shape and release

all sorts of built-up stresses, resulting in some disturbing sounds. Don't be perturbed by those sounds: if you don't do this now, it will happen while you're riding the bike, when it's too late to make the required corrections.

18. After stress-relieving, check the wheel for roundness and tightness once more—you will probably have to tighten several spokes a little more.

19. As you start riding, you'll probably hear all sorts of pinging coming from the spokes of the new wheel. It's nature's way of stress-relieving the spokes and "unwinding" twisted spokes, forced that way by the operation of screwing the nipples on tightly. After perhaps 40 km (25 miles) of cycling, re-tension the spokes and true the wheel once more.

Left: Fig. 8.11. Wheel in truing stand.

Right: Fig. 8.12. Use of wheel centricity gauge.

9
DERAILLEUR GEAR MAINTENANCE

Most adult bikes are equipped with derailleur gearing, and this chapter addresses its maintenance. The derailleur system consists of a rear derailleur and a front derailleur which move the chain sideways over a number of differently sized chainwheels and cogs to achieve different gear ratios.

DERAILLEUR OPERATION

The rear derailleur selects one of 7 to 10 cogs on the freewheel with different numbers of teeth, and the front derailleur selects one of 2 or 3 different size chain-rings.

Gear selection is made with shifters, which are either on the handlebars or on the frame's downtube. Most modern road bikes are shifted by means of ratcheted levers integrated with the brake levers, although sepa-rate shifters for downtube instal-lation are still available. Mountain bikes and other machines with flat handlebars are either shifted by means of shift levers mounted under the handlebars, just in-board from the brake levers, or rotating twist-grips or twist-rings integrated with the handgrips.

Think of derailleur gearing as an integral system: If there is a

Left: Fig. 9.1. Derailleur gearing in highest gear—largest chainring, smallest sprocket.

Above: Fig. 9.2. In the lowest gear—small chainring, large sprocket.

problem, it may be due to any of a number of factors, ranging from the derailleur mechanism to the cable to the shifter—in fact, even the chain or the cogs and chainrings may be at fault. Keep that in mind when troubleshooting for gearing problems. None of the components require much in the way of maintenance other than keeping them clean and occasional adjustment.

This chapter covers only the derailleurs and their controls. The chainrings are described in Chapter 12, and the freewheel in Chapter 11.

As for terminology, this text adheres to U.S. nomenclature. In the U.K., the front derailleur is usually called a "changer," while the rear derailleur is referred to as a "mech," short for mechanism.

THE REAR DERAILLEUR

The rear derailleur consists of a metal cage with two little or pulleys over which the chain is guided, and a spring-tensioned parallelogram mechanism that moves the cage sideways to line up with the different cogs on the freewheel at the rear wheel hub. Note the various adjusting screws sticking out at different points and the adjusting barrel for the cable tension.

The two most common problems at the rear derailleur are over- or undershifting and failure to index properly at the gear selected. Both these problems can usually be overcome with simple adjustments.

Above: Fig. 9.4. Changing up, with the rear derailleur forcing the chain to a smaller cog.

Left: Fig. 9.3. Changing down, with the rear derailleur forcing the chain to a larger cog.

Overshifting occurs when the chain is shifted too far in the highest or the lowest gear, getting caught between the smallest cog and the frame or between the biggest cog and the spokes. Undershifting occurs when the chain doesn't get shifted far enough at the smallest or the biggest cog, so the corresponding gear cannot be engaged.

Failure to index properly occurs when the chain doesn't line up with the cog, so the gear does not engage correctly—either skipping gears or running in gear with a scraping noise. The most common problem, improper indexing, is adjusted easily with the cable adjusting barrel at the point where the cable enters the derailleur.

ADJUST REAR DERAILLEUR

When the gears do not engage properly, first make sure the cable is in good condition. Clean, lubricate, or replace it if it isn't. This may solve the problem. If not, proceed as follows:

TOOLS & EQUIPMENT:

- Usually none required (sometimes an Allen wrench and pliers).

PROCEDURE:

1. Place the bike in an intermediate gear.

2. Locate the adjusting mechanism at the point where the

control cable enters the derailleur.

3. Turn the adjuster out in ½-turn increments and try shifting through the entire range of gears while turning the cranks with the wheel lifted off the ground. Note whether gear engagement gets better or worse.

   • If it got better, continue adjusting in small increments until the derailleur indexes properly.

   • If it got worse, turn the adjuster in the opposite direction until the derailleur indexes properly.

4. If you can't turn the adjuster in or out far enough:

   • Use the additional adjuster at the shifter or on the frame's downtube.

• Select the highest gear, i.e. the smallest cog, then clamp the cable in at a different point with the Allen wrench, using the pliers to pull the cable taut.

5. If the highest or lowest gear cannot be reached properly, or the chain shifts beyond the gear, refer to *Rear Derailleur Over- and Undershift Adjustment.*

ANGLE ADJUSTMENT NOTE:

On most derailleurs, there is a separate adjustment screw near the derailleur mounting point to adjust the limiting angle of the derailleur cage relative to the horizontal plane (referred to as "angle of dangle"). You may try adjusting this one way or the other, bringing the chain and the upper pulley (the jockey wheel) closer to, or farther from, the cogs.

REAR DERAILLEUR OVER- & UNDER-SHIFT ADJUSTMENT

This problem is particularly prevalent after the rear wheel or the cogs on the rear wheel have been replaced. However, it can also be due to normal wear or accidental damage.

Left: Fig. 9.5. Adjusting the rear derailleur.

Right: Fig. 9.6. Adjusting the rear the derailleur's "Angle of dangle."

TOOLS & EQUIPMENT:

• small Phillips screwdriver

PROCEDURE:

1. Find the two small adjusting screws that limit the sideways travel of the derailleur cage. Usually, one is marked "H" for high, limiting travel toward the high gear (outside, smallest cog), the other one "L" for low, limiting travel toward the low gear (inside, biggest cog).

   • If they're not marked, place the bike in the highest or the lowest gear (smallest or biggest cog) and establish which is which by turning one of them in (clockwise) to find out whether that results in less movement to the outside (so that would be "H") or the inside (so that would be "L").

2. Depending on the problem, turn the relevant adjusting screw in or out in ½-turn increments:

• Turn the "H" screw in to compensate for overshifting at the high gear (i.e. the chain was shifted beyond the smallest cog), or out to compensate for undershifting at the high end (i.e. the chain did not quite reach the smallest cog).

• Turn the "L" screw in to compensate for overshifting at the low gear (i.e. the chain was shifted beyond the largest cog), or out to compensate for undershifting at the low end (i.e. the chain did not quite reach the largest cog).

3. Lift the wheel off the ground and turn the crank, shifting into all the gears. If needed. fine-tune the adjustment until

the chain runs smoothly in all gears.

• Also see the *Angle adjustment note* above.

REAR DERAILLEUR MAINTENANCE

Before starting with this work, you may want to undo the cable attachment at the derailleur—however, then you'll have to readjust the system afterward. Usually, the work can be done with the derailleur still attached to its cable.

TOOLS & EQUIPMENT:

• Allen wrenches (or regular wrenches for older models)

• cloths

• solvent and lubricant

PROCEDURE:

1. Remove the bolt that holds the lower pulley (the tension wheel).

2. Remove the tension wheel; now the chain can be re-

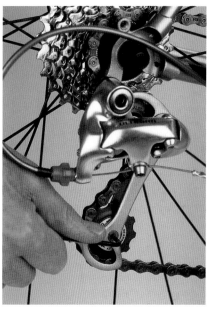

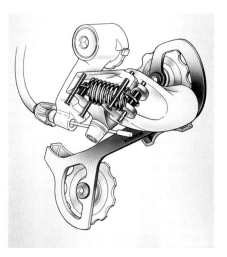

Above: Fig. 9.8. Manufacturer's illustration showing the rear derailleur's inner workings.

Left: Fig. 9.7. Rear derailleur over-and undershift adjustment.

Top right: Fig. 9.9. Removing or installing the rear derailleur pulleys

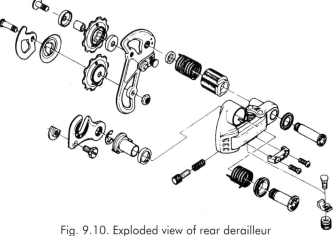

Fig. 9.10. Exploded view of rear derailleur

moved from the derailleur cage.

3. Also remove the other pulley (the jockey wheel).

4. Clean, inspect, and lubricate all parts. Replace the pulleys if they can't be made to turn freely.

5. Reinstall the jockey wheel.

6. Put the chain back in the cage.

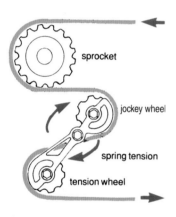

Fig. 9.11. Chain routing at rear derailleur.

7. Install the tension wheel.

8. Check operation and make any adjustments necessary.

REPLACE REAR DERAILLEUR

Usually, the rear derailleur is held by means of an Allen bolt, which attaches it to an extension of the right-side dropout called "derailleur eye." On low-end bikes, it may be attached to a separate mounting plate held between the hub and the dropout. Make sure the new derailleur is designed for the particular range of cogs on your wheel. To handle big gearing steps, you need a wide-range derailleur, characterized by a long cage—with the pulleys far apart.

Above: Fig. 9.13. Tension wheel and bearing exposed on a long-cage mountain bike derailleur.

Left: Fig. 9.12. Clamping in the rear derailleur cable, while holding it taut with pliers.

Right: Fig. 9.14. Removing or installing a rear derailleur.

TOOLS & EQUIPMENT

• Allen wrenches, and sometimes (for older derailleurs) a 7 mm open-ended or box wrench.

REMOVAL PROCEDURE:

1. Put the rear derailleur in the highest gear (smallest cog) and remove the cable, following the procedure for cable replacement on page 75.

2. Remove the jockey wheel to free the chain (alternately, you can disconnect the chain, following the procedure in Chapter 13).

3. Remove the mounting bolt, and take the derailleur off the bike.

INSTALLATION PROCEDURE:

1. Install the mounting bolt while pushing the derailleur up against the spring tension so

that it clears the derailleur eye (or the mounting plate).

2. If necessary, remove the tension wheel, then slide the chain in, and reinstall the tension wheel.

3. Attach the cable.

4. Make any adjustments that may be necessary, following the procedures above.

THE FRONT DERAILLEUR

The front derailleur is mounted on the seat tube. It comprises a simple cage through which the chain runs, shifted sideways by means of a parallelogram mechanism connected to the left-side shifter by means of a cable. There are two types: those operated from above and those operated from below. Installation is either with a clamp that fits around the seat tube or bolted to a mounting bracket welded to the seat tube.

ADJUST FRONT DERAILLEUR

When the gears do not engage properly in the front, first make sure the cable is in good condition (and replace it if it isn't). Then proceed to adjust.

TOOLS & EQUIPMENT:

• Usually none required (sometimes an Allen wrench and pliers).

PROCEDURE:

1. Select the gear that combines the middle chainring with an intermediate cog.

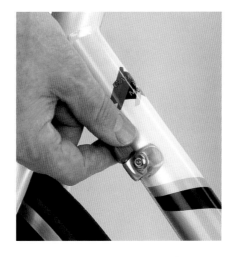

Above: Fig. 9.16. On most road bikes with integrated brake-shift lever, the front derailleur can be adjusted with this type of adjuster mounted on the down tube.

Left: Fig. 9.15. Front derailleur, shown here on a mountain bike with the derailleur clamped around the seat tube.

Right: Fig. 9.17. Additional adjustment is achieved by clamping in the cable at a different point.

2. Locate the adjusting mechanism at the point where the control cable enters the derailleur.

3. Turn the adjuster out in ½-turn increments, and try shifting through the entire range of gears, turning the cranks with the wheel lifted off the ground. Note whether shifting gets better or worse.

• If it got better, continue adjusting in ½-turn increments until the chain engages the chainrings properly.

• If it got worse, turn the adjuster in the opposite direction until the chain engages the chainrings properly.

4. If there is not enough adjustment to solve the problem:

• Use the additional adjuster at the shifter that may be present on bikes with flat handlebars.

• If still no luck, elect the highest gear, i.e. the largest chain-

ring, then clamp the cable in at a different point with the wrench, using the needle-nose pliers to pull the cable taut.

5. If the highest or lowest gear cannot be reached properly, or the chain shifts beyond the gear, refer to *Over- and Undershift Adjustment* below.

FRONT DERAILLEUR OVER- & UNDERSHIFT ADJUSTMENT

When this problem occurs, the chain gets stuck beyond the small or the big chainring (overshift), or it can't be shifted onto one of the chainrings (undershift). It may either be due to normal wear or accidental damage.

TOOLS & EQUIPMENT:

• small Phillips screwdriver

PROCEDURE:

1. Find the two small adjusting screws on top, which limit the

sideways travel of the front derailleur cage. Usually, one is marked "H" for high, limiting travel toward the high gear (outside, large chainring), the other one "L" for low, limiting travel toward the low gear (inside, small chainring). If they're not marked, establish which is which by turning one of them in (clockwise) to find out whether that results in less movement to the inside (so that would be "L") or the outside (so that would be "H").

2. Depending on the problem, turn the relevant adjusting screw in or out in ½-turn increments:

• Turn the "H" screw in to compensate for overshifting at

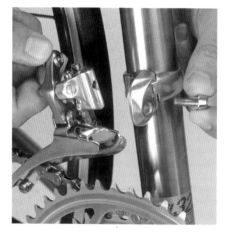

Above: Fig. 10.19. The front derailleur is installed on the seat tube, just above the chainrings.

Left: Fig. 10.18. Front derailleur over- or undershift adjustment.

Right: Fig. 10.20. Tightening or loosening the front derailleur mounting bolt.

the high gear (i.e. the chain was shifted beyond the largest chainring), or out to compensate for undershifting at the high end (i.e. the chain did not quite reach the largest chainring).

• Turn the "L" screw in to compensate for overshifting at the low gear (i.e. the chain was shifted beyond the smallest chainring), or out to compensate for undershifting at the low end (i.e. the chain did not quite reach the smallest chainring).

3. Lift the wheel off the ground and turn the cranks, shifting the front derailleur to each of the chainrings. If required, fine- tune the adjustment until the chain runs smoothly in all gears.

REPLACE FRONT DERAILLEUR

Front derailleurs are either mounted with a clamp that fits around the seat tube or directly on a tab that's welded to the seat

tube. Either way, they'll be held with an Allen bolt on modern bikes, while on older bikes it may be a conventional hexagonal-head bolt and nut.

TOOLS & EQUIPMENT:

- Allen wrenches (or whatever kind of wrenches fit)
- screwdriver to open up the derailleur cage to remove the chain

REMOVAL PROCEDURE:

1. Remove the little screw that holds the two sides of the derailleur cage together so you can remove the chain (or, if it cannot easily be opened, disconnect the chain, following the instructions in Chapter 14).

2. Undo the cable.

3. Remove the mounting bolt and remove the derailleur.

INSTALLATION PROCEDURE:

1. Open up the derailleur cage, and close it again with the chain in between. If that's not practical, open up the chain and place it through the cage, then close up the chain again.

2. If the derailleur gets clamped around the seatpost, place the derailleur clip around the seatpost. Otherwise, attach it to the mounting plate. Don't quite tighten it yet.

3. Most front derailleurs are set to engage the smallest

chainring in this position. A few models engage the largest one in this "default" mode (i.e. when the cable is not pulling it). Establish which way it is.

4. Align the cage parallel to the chainrings, leaving about 1/8–1/4 in. (3–6 mm) between the cage and the chainring (biggest or smallest depending on type). Then tighten the bolt in further with the wrench.

5. Attach the cable and adjust it so the derailleur is aligned with the "default" chainring when the cable is just taut but not tensioned.

6. Place the chain on the appropriate chainring.

Above: Fig. 9.21. Lifting the derailleur cable in or out of the cable stop.

Right: Fig. 9.22. Ratcheted front derailleur cable tension adjuster.

7. Check operation of the gears and make any adjustments necessary.

REPLACE DERAILLEUR CABLE

Replace the cable if it is hard to move, either because it is corroded or damaged— pinched, kinked, or frayed. Whether for the front or the rear derailleur, the procedure is the same.

If it's an indexed derailleur, buy a cable for the particular derailleur on your bike (yes, nowadays they're quite specific); if not, just make sure it's a cable with the right type of nipple (check at the shifter what shape and size it has). Before you start, put the bike in the gear that engages the smallest cog in the rear or the smallest chainring in the front.

TOOLS & EQUIPMENT:

- wrench for cable clamp at derailleur
- needle-nose pliers

- cable cutters

- sometimes diagonal cutters

- cloth and lubricant (preferably wax)

PROCEDURE:

1. Undo the cable clamp bolt at the derailleur.

2. At the shifter, pull the outer cable back a little and then push the inner cable in toward the shifter to expose the nipple at the shifter and enough cable to reach that point with the pliers.

3. Pull the cable out, first with the pliers, then by hand, catching the various sections of outer cable at the shifter and at the derailleur.

4. Make sure the new cable and the outer cable sections are of the same type and length as the original. Then apply some lubricant to the inner cable.

5. Starting at the shifter, install the inner cable through the

shifter, the outer cable sections, over or through any guides on the frame, and into the derailleur itself.

6. Clamp the cable end provisionally (i.e. not too tight yet).

7. Try the gears, turning the cranks with the wheel lifted off the ground, and adjust the cable (both with the adjuster and with the cable clamp bolt) until all gears work properly—refer to the relevant procedures *Adjust Rear Derailleur* or *Adjust Front Derailleur*.

SHIFTER MAINTENANCE

There's not much you can do on modern integrated shifters: they either work or they have to be replaced. If your bike is equipped with separately mounted shifters, you can simply take them apart and see whether there's something damaged or, more typically, loose, dirty, or corroded.

Fix what you find to be wrong and tighten the bolt that holds everything together when done. Adjust the relevant derailleur after such work, and chances are you've taken care of the problem. If not, you'll just have to replace the shifter.

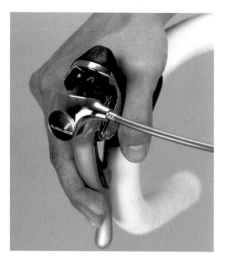

Above: Fig. 9.24. Typical mountain bike shift lever.

Left: Fig. 9.23. Integrated brake-shift lever, shown with the brake lever depressed to expose the mechanism.

Top right: Fig. 9.25. Down-tube shift lever, showing how the cable is installed.

Bottom right: Fig. 9.26. Handlebar-end shifter, as used on many touring and randonneur bikes.

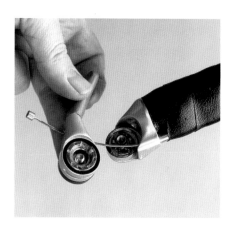

10
HUB GEAR MAINTENANCE

Although it's long been looked down upon by "serious" cyclists, hub gearing is now gaining popularity. It is only marginally less efficient than derailleur gearing, and it does offer some practical advantages, especially for city bikes.

WHY HUB GEARING?

With the mechanism hidden inside the wheel hub, it's less sensitive to damage and the ravages of the weather, which makes it a good choice in areas where people actually *use* their bikes for everyday transportation. It's also easier to use, trading the many options available on a derailleur system for fewer, but more easily selected gears.

HYBRID GEARING SYSTEMS

In addition to straightforward hub gearing, it's also possible to use a hybrid system. In this case, a hub gear is used in combination with a rear derailleur. Another hybrid option, though not strictly a hub gear, is the Mountain Drive 2-speed gear built into the crankset, replacing the front derailleur. Hybrid systems lend themselves well for use on folding and recumbent bicycles.

The major manufacturers of hub gearing are Shimano, SRAM (formerly Sachs), and Sturmey-Archer (which is now just a brand name owned by Sun-Race of Taiwan). All three major manufacturers have in recent years done much to widen the range of available gears on their hub gearing systems.

Left: Fig. 10.1. Drive train of bike with hub gear.

Right: Fig; 10.2. Typical modern hub gear.

HUB GEARING COMPONENTS

A straightforward hub gearing system consists of a gear mechanism contained in a special hub in the rear wheel, a shifter mounted on the handlebars, and a control cable. The hub typically offers anywhere from 2 to 8 different gearing stages.

The finest—and most expensive—hub gear is a 14-speed hub by the German Rohloff company. And a company called Fallbrook Technologies has just introduced their NuVinci infinitely variable transmission hub, which works on its own distinct principle—but it may take some time before

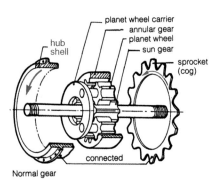

Normal gear

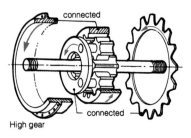

High gear

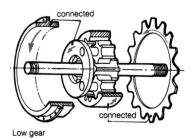

Low gear

Fig. 10.3. Hub gear operation diagram.

you'll encounter it on production bikes.

The conventional gear hub contains one or more planetary drive systems that are too complex to describe here. However, their function is straightforward: depending on the gear selected, their single cog turns faster or slower than the hub (and hence slower than the wheel itself). When the wheel turns slower than the cog, you're in a low gear; when both turn at the same speed, you've got the "normal" gear; and when the wheel turns faster than the cog, you're in a high gear.

The shifter is either in the form of a lever (or sometimes two separate levers) mounted on the handlebars or a twist grip or twist ring mounted inboard of the fixed handgrip.

The control cable connects the shifter with a selector mechanism on the side of the hub (usually on the right, but it can be either side, or even on both sides).

Although hybrid gearing systems often use a freewheel cassette with several cogs on the rear wheel, normal hub gears come with only a single cog,

Right: Fig. 10.4. Manufacturer's cut-away view of modern multi-speed hub gear, this one with a built-in coaster brake.

which is held on to the hub with splines and a spring clip. Removing the spring clip allows you to replace the cog.

The gear hub is often combined with a brake. That may be a coaster brake, a drum brake, or a roller brake. Operation of the coaster brake is by pedaling back, while drum and roller brakes are controlled by a brake lever on the handlebars via a cable (or sometimes pull rods). See Chapter 17 for more information on these brakes.

If you have to remove such a wheel from the bike for maintenance, you'll have to disconnect the brake counter-lever and the brake control cable as well as the gear control cable itself—and install and adjust them again afterward.

HUB GEAR MAINTENANCE

If bought new, these hubs come with an instruction manual that deals with basic handling and adjusting. If you got one, refer to it, because the instructions there will be more specific to the make and model in question. If not, here are

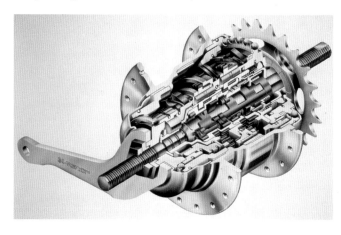

some tips to help you on your way.

When a hub gearing system does not work properly, it's usually something that can be alleviated with adjusting. If that doesn't do the job, you may well be faced with having to replace one of the system components—the shifter, the control cable, or the hub itself.

Keeping the various components clean and lightly lubricated is your major line of defense against hub gear trouble.

Gear malfunctions usually show up as a failure to shift into a specific gear properly; sometimes none of the gears can be engaged, with the chain apparently slipping.

The first thing to check is the cable: make sure it is not damaged or pinched anywhere. Next, try simple adjusting. All hub gear systems come with an adjusting device—either at the shifter or at the hub.

HUB GEAR ADJUSTMENT

TOOLS & EQUIPMENT:

- Usually none required.

PROCEDURE:

1. Set the shifter for the highest gear while rotating the crank with the rear wheel off the ground.

2. Check the point where the cable is attached to the control mechanism at the hub: in the selected position, it should be just slack, i.e. without tension. However, as soon as you shift down, it should become taut and the hub should engage the next gear as you move it

Above: Fig. 10.7. Sturmey-Archer adjustment at the point where the cable connects to the selector control.

Top Left: Fig. 10.5. SRAM's twist-grip control for their multi-speed hub gear.

Bottom left: Fig. 10.6. SRAM's "click box" adjuster at the interface between cable and control mechanism.

Right: Fig. 10.8. Adjusting gear selector controls on a Shimano hub gear.

to the next setting at the shifter.

3. If it doesn't shift properly, turn the adjuster in (to loosen) half a turn at a time and check whether the situation improves. If not, turn it out in similar increments.

SRAM NOTE:

These hubs (and their Sachs predecessors) are equipped with an ingenious adjusting clip referred to as a "Click Box." Instead of a conventional adjusting barrel, there is a little metal or plastic bracket with a spring clip, into which the threaded adjusting pin is pushed and held in place. Easy to connect, to disconnect, and to adjust: just push the clip while pulling the threaded pin all the way out, then insert the pin again until the cable tension is right.

GENERAL NOTE:

On some hub gears, the control that projects from the hub is a little chain (especially on older hubs). In case of malfunction, it may be either too loose or turned in under such an angle that it is kinked. In the first case, undo the connection with the cable, and

screw the control into the hub a little tighter; then reattach the cable. In the second case, undo and loosen it a little so it is not kinked; then reattach it to the cable.

ADDITIONAL MAINTENANCE SUGGESTIONS

If the problem can't be alleviated with simple adjusting, see what you can do with the following suggestions:

1. Clean and lightly lubricate all parts—hub, cog(s), chain, control mechanism, cable, and shifter.

2. Check whether it's really is a malfunction in the system itself (although that usually is the cause, you don't want to be barking up the wrong tree if it isn't). Make sure the chain is properly tensioned, the wheel properly positioned, and the chainring and cog(s) engage the chain properly.

3. Next, check to make sure the cable is in good condition; free it if it is caught somewhere along the way, lubricate

it if it is dry, and replace it if it is kinked or frayed.

4. Loosen the control cable, and check whether the shifter works smoothly when it is not attached to the hub. If it does not, see what you can do to make it work, or replace it with a new one.

5. If the problem does not get resolved this way, it's time to take the bike to a bike shop that has information on hub gears (at least in the U.S., these things are still too rare for every bike shop to be equipped for them—and even if they are, they may suggest just replacing the whole wheel instead of repairing the hub).

ADJUST GEAR RANGE

The gear range with which the hub-geared bike comes may not be to your liking. Often all the gears are too high or too low. In theory, you can make them lower or higher by replacing either the chainring or the cog by one of a different size. It'll be easiest to install a smaller or larger cog (smaller for higher gears, larger for lower gears). You'll have to adjust the rear wheel position or the

chain length to keep the chain snug on the cog—it should be possible to move the chain up or down by about 2 cm (¾ in.).

To replace the cog, remove the rear wheel, pry the spring clip out of its groove with a small screwdriver, and then lift out the cog, replace it with another one for that make and model of hub, and push the spring clip back into place. When working on the spring clip, hold it down with a cloth so it does not accidentally "jump" out at you.

If you're unhappy with the "width" of the gearing range, e.g. you find that the low gear is not low enough *and* the high gear not high enough, you don't have much choice—at best, you may be able to replace a 3-speed by a 7- or 8-speed hub, both of which do have a wider range (but that means a new hub, a rebuilt wheel, and a new shifter—difficult and expensive). So if you're really picky about your gears, only a derailleur system will offer the flexibility you're looking for.

Left: Fig. 10.9. The control mechanism on Shimano's 7- and 8-speed models is color-coded to assure correct orientation, e.g. when reinstalling the rear wheel.

Right: Fig. 10.10. Replacing the rear sprocket on a gear hub to achieve a different gear range.

11

FREEWHEEL & COG MAINTENANCE

The rear wheel cogs, or sprockets, are usually mounted on a freewheel mechanism. The freewheel contains a kind of ratcheting system to turn forward when driven without forcing the rider to be pedaling all the time, usually also allowing you to pedal back while the bike continues going forward or is standing still. Derailleur bikes have a whole range of cogs, while single-speed and hub-gear bikes have only one.

THE COGS

The cogs are either screwed on or held on splines and held together by means of a screwed-on item (either a separate lock ring or the smallest cog).

At least once a year, clean the cogs—and the spaces between them. To clean between the cogs, use a thin cloth folded into a narrow strip, stretched between both hands, going back and forth all around (it's easiest with the wheel removed off the bike). If dirt doesn't come off, soak the cloth in a mixture of solvent and 5–10% mineral oil.

Above: Fig. 11.1. Typical cassette freewheel unit for derailleur bikes.

Right: Fig. 11.2. Single-speed freewheel unit.

Individual cogs can be replaced by first removing the last, screwed-on item. This is done with a special tool—buy the appropriate tool for the type of freewheel on your bike if you want to do this work yourself. On cassette hubs, the choice of cogs is rather limited, in that they come in sets, and usually it will not be possible to pick different sequences of cogs, as can be done with the old-fashioned screwed-on freewheel block.

When replacing either an entire cassette or some of the cogs on a cassette, make sure they are compatible with that hub.

One reason you may want to replace one or more of the cogs would be in case of wear, causing shifting problems or chain skip. At that point, you should replace both the cog in question (usually the smallest one) *and* the chain, because the old, "stretched" chain would no longer fit the tooth pattern on the new cog, which causes chain skip.

THE FREEWHEEL

The freewheel is either integrated in a portion of the hub (in the case of cassette hubs, hub gearing and single-speed systems) or in a separate unit that is screwed on to the hub.

The freewheel body can be lubricated with thick mineral oil (SAE 60) inserted in the visible gap between moving parts inside.

If the freewheel mechanism fails or becomes either too loose or starts to run "rough," it can be replaced. The method depends on whether it's

Above: Fig. 11.5. All cogs removed from splined Freehub body.

Top left: Fig. 11.3. Using a splined cog tool to remove the screwed-on smallest cog.

Bottom left: Fig. 11.4. Small cog and spacer removed, exposing splined cogs.

Top right: Fig. 11.7. Removing Freehub body from a cassette-type hub.

Below: Fig. 11.6. Freehub with the cogs removed.

the screwed-on type or the cassette type.

The screwed-on freewheel is removed with a special freewheel tool. Remove the wheel, hold the tool loosely with the wheel's quick-release skewer (or axle nuts), then unscrew it, using a large wrench, holding the wheel firmly. Gradually loosen the quick-release thumb nut (or axle nut) as needed along the way.

When replacing a screwed-on freewheel, clean and lubricate the screw thread, and screw the new freewheel on by hand.

The cassette freewheel is held on by means of a hollow internal 10 mm Allen bolt. It is accessible after you remove the axle and can be removed with a 10 mm Allen wrench as shown in Fig. 11.7.

When a spoke on the chain side of the rear wheel breaks, you

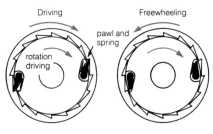

Fig. 11.8. Freewheel principle diagram.

have to remove the freewheel (in the case of a screwed-on freewheel block) or the cogs (in the case of a cassette hub). This is probably the most common reason to remove these items.

ADAPT GEAR RANGE

If the gears on your bike are not high enough or, more typically, not low enough, you can change that by replacing some cogs by bigger or smaller ones. To achieve a higher top gear, you could exchange either the smallest cog with a smaller one or the largest chain-

ring with a larger one. To achieve a lower low gear, replace either the biggest cog by a bigger one or the smallest chainring by a smaller one.

That's the theory. In practice, these days, cogs usually come "prepackaged" in certain combinations, and it may be hard or impossible to find an individual replacement cog to match your needs. Find out at a bike shop which combinations are available to satisfy your needs and exchange them accordingly—whether individually or as a set of several matching ones.

To exchange cogs, first remove the rear wheel. Then either unscrew the smallest cog that holds the rest together on a cassette hub, or use the chain whip to separate the cogs on a screwed-on freewheel. Put the new cog(s) in place and reinstall the wheel. If you

installed larger cogs, you may need a wide-range derailleur, with has a longer cage, with the pulleys farther apart, and a longer chain to accommodate them.

FIXED WHEELS & SINGLE SPEEDS

Recently there has been a resurgence of single-speed bikes, i.e. those without any gears at all. There are three types: with freewheel, without freewheel, and with a freewheel on one side of the hub and a "fixed" gear wheel on the other. The fixed wheel is screwed on and usually held with a lock ring with left-hand screw thread, as shown in Fig. 11.13. Maintenance is the same as it is for any other cog and/or screwed-on freewheel

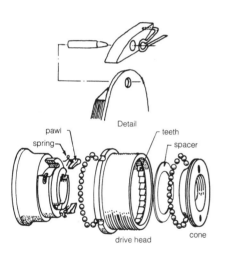

Fig. 11.9. Exploded view of freewheel mechanism.

Above: Fig. 11.12. Removing the screwed-on freewheel from a threaded hub.

Top left: Fig. 11.10. Use of special adapter tool to lubricate the freewheel mechanism.

Bottom left: fig. 11.11. This hub has a single-speed freewheel on one side and a fixed cog on other side.

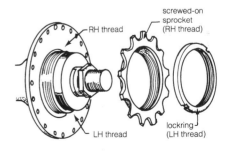

Fig. 11.13. Fixed sprocket installation detail.

12

CRANKSET MAINTENANCE

T he crankset, referred to as chain-set in Britain, consists of the bottom bracket (bearings and axle, or spindle), the cranks, or crank arms, and the chainrings that are attached to the right-side crank.

The crankset is part of the bicycle's overall transmission system, or drivetrain, together with the pedals, the chain, and the components of the gearing system.

THE CRANKS

Almost all modern bicycles come equipped with what is referred to

as cotterless cranks—as opposed to older bikes, especially cheaper ones, on which the cranks were attached by means of cotter pins. Although you'll also be shown how to deal with the latter, we'll

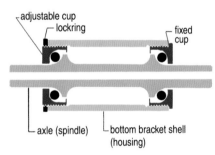

Fig. 12.4. Cross-section diagram of conventional (adjustable) bottom bracket.

Above: Fig. 12.2. Single-speed crankset.

Left: Fig. 12.1. Typical mountain bike crankset, with triple chainwheels. Road bike cranksets are similar but with only two chainrings.

Right: Fig. 12.3. Tandem crankset, with triple chainrings on the left and a single chainring on the left, that is connected to a front crankset with same size chainwheel.

start off with the now common cotterless cranks. They're almost invariably made of aluminum alloy—nice and light, but it does mean that the screw thread is quite sensitive and must be treated carefully.

The ends of the bottom bracket axle are either tapered in a square pattern or splined. The crank has a correspondingly patterned recess on the inside (i.e. the side facing the bike's frame).

On square-tapered models, each crank is held on by means of a bolt (or sometimes a nut), which sits in a larger recess facing out. Usually there's some kind of dust cap to cover the recess. The recess has internal screw thread, which allows removal of the cranks with a special tool.

Some cranksets have a clever "one-key-release" system on which the attachment bolt also serves as a crank puller. For these, you'll only require an 8 mm Allen wrench.

On splined models, the right-side crank is often permanently attached to the axle, while the left-side crank is split and

clamped around the splined axle end by means of two Allen bolts.

The right-side crank has a star-shaped device to which the chainrings are attached at 3, 4, or 5 points by means of small bolts and nuts.

At the end of the crank there is a hole with screw thread for the pedal. The right-side crank has regular right-hand screw thread, while the one on the left has left-hand screw thread (that's so the left pedal doesn't work loose as you pedal).

TIGHTEN CRANK

Do this work in conjunction with the monthly inspection, and whenever you hear or feel creaking or other signs of looseness in the connection between the crank and the bottom bracket. Proceed as follows:

TOOLS & EQUIPMENT:

• depending on crank type, wrench part of crank tool or

specific crank bolt wrench or Allen wrench

• tool to fit dust cap, if installed (depending on type, an Allen wrench, a pin wrench, a screwdriver, or a coin)

PROCEDURE FOR BIKES WITH LARGE EXPOSED ALLEN BOLT

This type is found on most modern bikes.

1. Tighten the Allen bolt with an 8 mm Allen wrench while holding the crank firmly for leverage.

2. Also tighten the other crank, even if it did not seem loose.

PROCEDURE FOR BIKES WITH SEPARATE METAL DUST CAP:

1. Remove the dust cap from the threaded recess in the crank.

2. Using the wrench part of the crank tool (or a specific crank bolt wrench), tighten the bolt while holding the crank firmly for leverage.

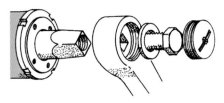

Fig. 12.5. Cotterless crank attachment, shown here with square tapered spindle.

Left: Fig. 12.6. Removing dustcap on crankset with concealed bolt.

Right: Fig. 12.7. Tightening crank on bike with exposed Allen bolt.

3. Reinstall the dust cap.

HOLLOWTECH NOTE:

On these hollow-spindle cranksets, the right-side crank arm with the chainrings is permanently attached to the (hollow) spindle. Only the left-side crank has to be tightened. It is split at the end and clamped around the splined, hollow spindle with two Allen bolts, one on each side. Keep these equally tightened, with moderate hand force.

To install, push the spindle back in and clamp the left-side crank back on with moderate hand force.

REMOVE & INSTALL CRANK

Do this work to gain access to the bottom bracket itself, e.g. for bearing overhaul, or to replace the crank. Also here, see the *Hollowtech note* for hollow spindle cranksets.

TOOLS & EQUIPMENT:

• crank tool (both the puller part and the crank bolt wrench part) and second wrench, or just an 8 mm Allen wrench (depending on the crank bolt type)

• for Hollowtech cranks: 5 mm Allen wrench

PROCEDURE:

1. Remove the dust cap and then the bolt—or the Allen bolt with a black plastic ring around it, or just loosen the Allen bolt (on splined-spindle models, which you'll recognize by the fact that there is a metal cap with two little round recesses around the 8 mm Allen bolt).

Above: Fig. 12.9. Hollowtech left-side crank and splined, split spindle.

Left: Fig. 12.8. Hollowtech crankset overview. The right-side crank is permanently attached to the bottom bracket spindle.

Right: Fig. 12.10. The left-side Hollowtech crank is clamped around the spindle with two Allen bolts.

• If the bolt or the nut comes out (non-splined-spindle models), remove any washer that may be present (very important: if you forget this step, you won't be able to pull the crank off—and ruin the screw thread in the crank).

• On splined spindle models, just keep turning the bolt loose (which after the first one or two turns becomes much harder to do—but persevere anyway), and it will pull the crank off the spindle.

2. On models requiring use of the crank extractor tool, make sure there is no washer left in the recess and the puller is fully retracted (i.e. the central threaded part does not project); then screw it into the threaded recess in the crank as far as possible, using the wrench.

3. Holding the outer part of the crank extractor tool with one wrench, screw in the central part with the other one.

4. The crank will be pulled off this way; then unscrew the tool from the crank.

INSTALLATION PROCEDURE:

1. Clean and inspect, and if necessary, replace parts; then apply a thin layer of grease (or preferably anti-seize lubricant) on the matching flat or splined surfaces of the bot-

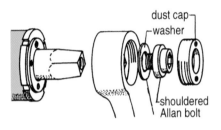

Fig. 12.11. One-key release system.

tom bracket spindle and the crank.

2. Place the crank on the bottom bracket spindle, making sure it's 180 degrees offset from the other crank, and push it on by hand as far as possible.

3. On non-splined-spindle models, install the washer, then the bolt, and tighten the bolt firmly, using the crank for leverage.

4. Tighten the bolt and then, only on non-splined-spindle models, install the dust cap or the plastic ring.

Above: Fig. 12.14. Pushing the crank off the spindle using crank puller and wrench.

Top left: Fig. 12.12. Splined crank and bottom bracket spindle.

Bottom left: Fig. 12.13. Installing crank bolt in square-taper bottom bracket spindle.

Right: Fig. 12.15. Use of crank puller tool.

5. After an hour's cycling, re-tighten the bolt; and once more after another 4 hours' use—and immediately anytime it seems to be getting loose (e.g. if you hear creaking sounds).

ONE-KEY CRANK ATTACHMENT NOTE:

If what looks like a dust cap around an 8 mm Allen bolt has two round recesses, it's probably the type with a one-key release. On these, loosening the Allen bolt far enough actually pushes the crank off. Don't remove the thing that looks like a dust cap (you'd have to use a pin wrench to do so) because it is actually a restraint against which the crank bolt pushes to remove the crank, and you would have a hard time removing the crank if it were gone.

COTTERED CRANKS

Though not en vogue on today's bikes, there are still some of these out there on older bikes, and they have to be maintained too. The

bottom bracket used on these is usually of the same type as the conventional one used with older cotterless cranks. So the only thing that's different is the attachment of the cranks to the bottom bracket axle.

If a cottered crank comes loose, it should be tightened immediately to prevent more damage. To tighten it, support the crank close to the nut that's screwed on to the cotter pin on something solid, and firmly hit the cotter pin from the other side with a mallet or a hammer (protecting it with a block of wood); then tighten the nut very firmly.

To remove a cottered crank (e.g. to gain access to the bearings), unscrew the nut and remove it with the underlying washer. Then, supporting the crank close to the cotter pin opposite the threaded side, place a thin block of hardwood on the end of the screw thread for protection and hit it hard with a hammer until the cotter pin comes loose and you can push it through with a screwdriver. (More elegantly, it can be done with a special tool that works like a C-clamp to push the cotter pin out.)

To reinstall a cottered crank, buy a new set of cotter pins of the right dimension. First clean and lightly grease all parts (the hole in the crank, the grooved section of the axle, and the cotter pin). Then install the cotter pin from the side of the crank with the larger diameter hole. Push the cotter pin in as far as possible, then hit it with a hammer while supporting the crank close to the hole. Install the washer and the nut and tighten the nut fully. Tighten the nut again after an hour's riding.

THE BOTTOM BRACKET

The bottom bracket is installed in the bottom bracket shell, i.e. the short piece of large-diameter tubing that runs perpendicular to the other tubes at the point where the seat tube, the downtube, and the chainstays come together. It is the most heavily loaded set of ball bearings of the bike. The cranks are attached on either side.

Above: Fig. 12.17. Loosening or tightening bottom bracket lockring and/or bearing using a pin wrench and a lockring tool.

Right: Fig. 12.18. Removing adjustable bearing cup.

These days, the bottom bracket is usually a self-contained unit, or cartridge, that gets installed in one piece. Older bottom brackets, and those on some cheaper bikes, may be of the type that has separate cup-and-cone bearings, which (unlike the bearings of a cassette-type bottom bracket) can be adjusted, lubricated, and overhauled. The latter type comes in several different varieties: the BSA-type, found on most older road bikes and mountain bikes, the one that's often referred to as Ashtabula that's found on old American cruisers and children's bikes, and the Thompson type used on some low-end bikes.

ADJUST, LUBRICATE, OR OVERHAUL BSA BOTTOM BRACKET

Do this work if the cup-and-cone bearings of a bottom bracket feel either loose or tight. If they're loose, adjusting may be enough, but if they're tight, you should also lubricate the bearings. Adjusting can be done with the cranks still attached, while the left-side crank must be removed

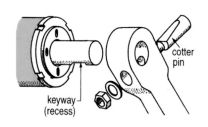

Fig. 12.16. Cottered crank attachment.

to lubricate or overhaul the bearings.

TOOLS & EQUIPMENT:

- special bottom bracket tools
- ball bearing grease and cloth (if the bearing is to be lubricated or overhauled)

ADJUSTING PROCEDURE:

1. Using the matching tool, unscrew the notched lockring on the left side of the bottom bracket by about one turn.

2. Using the pin wrench of the bottom bracket tools, tighten or loosen the left-side bearing cup about 1/8 turn.

3. Holding the bearing cup with the pin wrench, tighten the lockring firmly, making sure the bearing cup does not accidentally turn with it.

4. Check to make sure the adjustment is correct now and repeat if necessary.

DISASSEMBLY PROCEDURE:

1. After at least the left-side crank has been removed (preferably also the right-side crank, and if not, then at least remove the chain off the chainring before you start), use the matching tool to remove the lockring on the left side.

2. Using the pin wrench, remove the bearing cup on the left side.

3. Remove the bearing balls (usually held in a retainer) on the left side.

4. Pull out the bottom bracket axle from the right side, and catch the bearing balls (also usually in a retainer) on the right side. Also remove the plastic sleeve that's usually installed inside the bottom bracket shell to keep dirt from entering from the seat tube.

5. Unless you really want to replace the entire unit, stop here. Otherwise, also remove the bearing cup on the right side, using the matching tool. Beware that this bearing usually has left-hand screw thread (except on some French bikes), so you have to turn it clockwise to remove it.

OVERHAULING PROCEDURE:

1. Clean and inspect all components and replace any damaged, pitted, or corroded items (it's a good idea to replace the bearing balls, available both individually and as complete sets in retainers). The left-side bearing cup can be inspected while on the bike—use a flashlight (torch in U.K. vernacular) to see the condition of the bearing surface—but it would have to be removed and replaced if it is damaged or badly worn (see Step 5 of the disassembly procedure above).

2. Fill the bearing cups with bearing grease and make sure the screw threads of bottom bracket shell, bearing cup, and lockring are clean; then apply some lubricant (preferably anti-seize lubricant) to the screw-threads.

3. Insert the bearing balls with the retainer in the grease-filled bearing cups, with the closed side of the retainer facing into the bearing cup (facing out on the assembled bike).

Left: Fig. 12.19. The spindle with the right-side bearing balls installed and lubricated.

Right: Fig. 12.20. Lubricating the bearing cup.

4. Insert the bottom bracket axle from the left side, followed by the plastic sleeve that is usually installed inside the shell to keep dirt out of the bearings.

5. Screw the left-side bearing cup into the bottom bracket shell until the bearing is almost tight.

6. Screw the lockring over the left-side bearing cup and hold the latter with the pin wrench while tightening the lockring with the special wrench.

7. Check the bearing adjustment for smooth running before the cranks are installed, for play after the cranks are installed, and adjust if required.

REPLACE CARTRIDGE BEARING BOTTOM BRACKET

Do this work if a cartridge bearing bottom bracket is loose or does not turn smoothly. Both cranks must be removed first.

TOOLS & EQUIPMENT:

• special bottom bracket tool(s) for the make and model in question

• special lockring wrench

REMOVAL PROCEDURE:

1. Compare the two sides of the bottom bracket to check whether both sides have separate lockring screwed over the top of a screw-threaded bearing adaptor, or only one side, with a one-piece adaptor on the other side. If there's only one lockring, note whether it's on the left or the right side, and make sure you assemble/disassemble working from the side with the lockring.

2. Remove the lockring on the left side if it's a unit with two lockring or if it's a unit with the lockring on the left. If it's a single-lockring unit with the lockring on the right, remove that lockring.

3. Unscrew the second lockring (if there is a lockring on the other side as well).

4. Unscrew the body of the bearing unit:

• If it's a single-lockring unit, always from the side opposite the lockring.

• If it's a double-lockring unit, always from the right (chain side).

NOTE:

If working from the right, you'll usually be dealing with left-hand thread (so you have to turn clockwise to remove, counterclockwise to install).

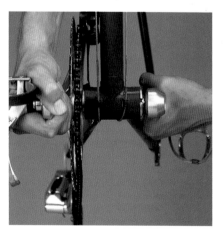

Left: Fig. 12.21. Checking bottom bracket bearing adjustment.

Above: Fig. 12.22. Bottom bracket unit with "sealed" cartridge bearing units instead of cup-and-cone bearings.

Right: Fig. 12.23. Removing a cartridge bottom bracket unit with a splined tool.

INSTALLATION PROCEDURE:

1. Make sure the new unit is designed for the same configuration as the old one and has the same axle length.

2. Clean and lightly lubricate (preferably with anti-seize lubricant) all screw threads, both in the bottom bracket shell and on the cartridge unit.

3. Screw the unit in from the side for which it is designed (usually from the left):

   • If it's a single-lockring type, until the flange on the cartridge is hard up against the face of the bottom bracket shell.

   • If it's a double-lockring type, until the thread projects equally far on both sides.

4. Install the lockring (or both lockrings if it's a double-lockring model) and tighten

well, holding the body of the unit with the matching pin wrench.

5. If it's a model with two lockrings, adjust the amount of projection on the two sides to be well balanced or to get as close as possible to the most direct chain line (as described in Chapter 13).

ONE-PIECE CRANKSET

This type is found mainly on American cruisers and low-end BMX and other children's bikes. As the name implies, the two crank arms are combined, together with the axle, as a single Z-shaped forged steel unit. They have to be adjusted about once a year, and whenever the bearings feel loose or tight.

TOOLS & EQUIPMENT:

• screwdriver

• wrench to fit locknut

PROCEDURE:

1. Loosen the locknut on the left side turning clockwise (left-hand thread).

2. Lift the keyed washer that lies underneath and then use the screwdriver to adjust the cone—to the left to tighten, to the right to loosen the bearing.

3. Holding the cone in place with the screwdriver, tighten the locknut counterclockwise.

NOTES:

• If the unit needs to be lubricated, you can gain access to the bearings by unscrewing the locknut and the cone all the way. At this point, you can push the Z-shaped unit out to the chain side of the bottom bracket shell, exposing the right-side bearing. Clean all

Left: Fig. 12.24. Cartridge bearing bottom bracket unit ready to be installed.

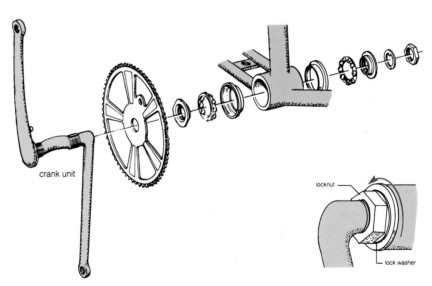

crank unit

locknut

lock washer

Fig. 12.25. One-piece, or "Ashtabula," crankset and adjusting detail.

parts before lubricating with grease. Then assemble again. To do this job more thoroughly, you'd have to remove the left-side pedal, which allows you to push the whole unit out to the chain side, giving you a chance to thoroughly clean, inspect, lubricate, and/or replace individual components.

- On these one-piece cranks, the chainring is held onto a threaded portion of the crank arm unit with a nut and an engagement peg on the inside of the right-side crank arm. Undo the nut to remove the chainring.

THOMPSON-TYPE BOTTOM BRACKET

This type, mainly found on some low-end European bikes, is shown in Fig. 12.24. To adjust the bearings, first loosen the locknut on the left side by turning clockwise (left-hand thread). Then turn the underlying dust cap, which engages the cone underneath—to the right to loosen, to the left to tighten the bearings.

If you need to gain access to the bearings, the cranks must be removed first. Then unscrew and remove the locknut, the washer, and the cone, after which the entire unit will come out on the chain side. Do the usual cleaning, inspection, and lubrication, and reassemble in reverse order, keeping in mind that the screw thread is left-handed.

THE CHAINRINGS

On derailleur bicycles, two or three chainrings, or chainwheels, are installed on the right-side crank. They usually come in a standard combination with respect to the numbers of teeth. They must be designed for the particular make and model of the crankset, because the number of attachment bolts, as well as the distance between them, can differ quite a bit.

Above: Fig. 12.27. Typical chainring unit as attached to the right-side crank, this one for mountain bike use.

Under normal circumstances, the chainrings do not wear very much and will hold up quite long. However, they may have to be replaced if they see a lot of hard use, especially in bad weather and muddy terrain—or if they get damaged. On non-derailleur bikes, there's only one chainring, and it's often permanently attached to the right-side crank (in which case it can only be replaced together with the crank, following the instructions above for crank replacement).

TIGHTEN CHAINRINGS

In conjunction with the annual inspection (and preferably even the monthly inspection), the chainrings may have to be tightened if one or more of the installation bolts is loose. It's also one of the possible causes for unpredictable shifting of derailleur gears.

TOOLS & EQUIPMENT:

- Allen wrenches (for older types, also a slotted wrench specifically designed to fit the attachment bolts)

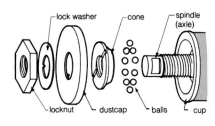

Fig. 12.26. Thompson type bottom bracket unit

Right: Fig. 12.28. Tightening chainring attachment bolts.

PROCEDURE:

1. Holding each of the bolts in the back of the chainring in turn with the slotted wrench, tighten the corresponding Allen bolt from the front, gradually working around until all bolts (usually four or five) have been tightened.

   • Replace any bolts that cannot be tightened with new ones (both parts of the bolt).

   • On triple-chainring units, there is usually a second set of bolts, accessible only from the back, holding the smallest chainring—check and tighten those bolts as well.

REPLACE CHAINRINGS

Do this if a chainring is damaged or worn. Or you may want to replace them with bigger or smaller ones or you may want to remove them for a more thorough cleaning. Do this work either with the right-side crank still installed on the bike or with the crank removed. Before you start, lift the chain off the chainring and place

it on the inside (i.e. between the chainring and the frame's seat tube.

TOOLS & EQUIPMENT:

• Allen wrench and a slotted wrench specifically designed to fit the attachment bolts

REMOVAL PROCEDURE:

1. Holding each of the bolts in the back of the chainring in turn with one Allen key or the slotted wrench, loosen the corresponding Allen bolt from the front, removing both parts, gradually working around until all bolts have been removed.

   • On triple-chainring units, there is usually a second set of bolts, accessible only from the back, holding the smallest chainring—remove those bolts as well. If not, the whole set of three chainrings stays together as a unit.

Left: Fig. 12.30. Chainring attachment bolt ready to install.

Above: Fig. 12.31. A single-speed's single chainring attachment detail.

2. Remove the chainrings, either separately (in which case there will also be spacers to catch) or as a unit.

INSTALLATION PROCEDURE:

1. Compare with the original configuration how the unit is assembled (you may have to do that before installing them to the crank's chainring attachment arms).

2. Attach one bolt (with spacer) and the other part of the bolt holding the chainring(s) to the attachment, but do not tighten it fully yet.

3. Do the same with another bolt roughly opposite the first one.

4. Install the remaining bolts.

5. Gradually tighten all bolts fully from the front, holding them in the back.

NOTES:

• Replace any bolts that cannot be tightened fully, making sure they're the right length.

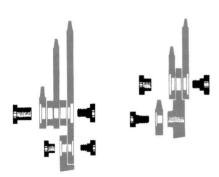

Fig. 12.29. Chainring attachment details.

- On bikes with special tooth patterns (these days, that's usually the case), the chainrings have to stay lined up the same way (because they're shaped that way to aid shifting). Check for an alignment mark to install them correctly.

STRAIGHTEN CHAINRING & CHAINRING TEETH

If either the chainring or one or more of the teeth are bent, you may be able to correct the situation by bending it back. But replace the whole chainring (or the whole riveted-together set of chainrings, if that's the way they come on your bike) if a tooth breaks or is permanently deformed—or when the chainring itself is so seriously bent that the tool won't straighten it. Before you start, lift the chain off the chainring to the inside.

TOOLS & EQUIPMENT:

- special chainring or chainring tooth tool (or in a pinch, an adjustable wrench)

PROCEDURE:

1. Fit the tool exactly over the tooth or the bent section of

Left: Fig. 12.32. Straightening individual bent chainring teeth.

Right: Fig. 12.33. Straightening bent chainring.

chainring as far as it will go without also grabbing beyond the location of the bend, and then use it to gradually straighten the tooth or the chainring.

2. Check the result and repeat if necessary. Replace the entire chainring(s) if a tooth remains seriously bent, cracks, or breaks—or if the chainring just can't be straightened.

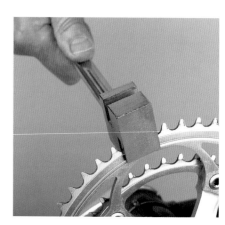

13

CHAIN MAINTENANCE

The bicycle chain consists of an array of chain links, connected by means of pins. Each neighboring set of link pins is connected with side plates, and there are bushings around the pins to reduce the friction.

CHAIN SIZES & TYPES

Chain size designation references the length and inside width of a link, measured between subsequent links and inside the inner side plates respectively. Derailleur bicycles take chains of the nominal dimension $\frac{1}{2}$ x $\frac{3}{32}$ inch, while non-derailleur bikes, especially those with coaster brakes, usually take the slightly wider chains of nominal dimension $\frac{1}{2}$ x $\frac{1}{8}$ inch.

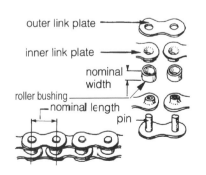

Fig. 13.1. Chain details.

The dimension of the derailleur chain is no longer as standardized as it once was. With the advent of 8-, 9-, and 10-speed freewheels, there is less space between them to accommodate a $\frac{3}{32}$ in. wide chain, so chains for these are narrower and identified by their inside width in mm.

When replacing a chain, or when adding links to an existing chain, it will be very important to get one that is identical, and that may involve not only the width, but also the design of the chain. The big word to keep in mind is "Hyperglide"—that's the standard for Shimano's narrow specially-shaped freewheel cogs, and the chain for bikes thus equipped must be "Hyperglide compatible." It does not have to be a chain made by Shimano, because Hyperglide-compatible

chains from other manufacturers work just as well.

The way the ends of the chain are connected differs for the two types: the wider chain for non-derailleur bikes is joined by means of a so-called master link, as shown in Figs. 13.11, while the narrower derailleur chain is joined the same way as in which all the pins connect subsequent links. To connect or disconnect the derailleur chain, one of the pins is pushed out far enough to free the inside link plate and back in again. To shorten a chain, a pin is pushed out all the way, so the last one or more links on the other side of that pin just drop out.

Above: Fig. 13.2. The chain running on the chainring in front.

CHAIN LINE

That's the path the chain takes relative to the centerline through the length of the bike. It's least troublesome when the chain runs exactly parallel. In reality, it will vary quite a bit from this "ideal" chain line when you shift gears on a derailleur bike, making it marginally less efficient. To keep these variations to an acceptable minimum (and more importantly, to aid gear shifting), the chain should preferably be run so that it follows the ideal chain line when the center between the two or three chainrings is lined up with the center between the biggest and smallest cog in the back.

GENERAL CHAIN MAINTENANCE

As far as chain maintenance is concerned, the main things to consider are cleaning, lubrication, and the amount of wear (which leads to apparent "stretch"). If you ride off-road a lot, the chain should probably be replaced every six months or so; otherwise, once a year should be enough for 10-speed chains, or once every 2–3 years for wider ones.

To check for wear, recommended at least once a year, use either a special chain wear tool or measure a 50-link section of chain to see whether it has apparently stretched. Replace the chain if the 50 links have stretched to the point where it's 25½ inches, rather than the 25 inches a new 50-link section would measure.

The best way to clean a chain is to remove it and rinse it out in a mixture of solvent with 5–10% mineral oil, brushing and rinsing it thoroughly. Then hang it out to dry, and once dry, lubricate it. In dry climates, the best lubricants are wax-based, whereas in wet weather, grease-based lubricants work best for the chain. The easiest way to apply the lubricant is with a spray can or a special dispenser with a brush at the end.

As a result of an accident or maltreatment of the bike (e.g.

when transporting or storing it), one or more links of a chain may be bent or twisted. This will seriously affect shifting on a derailleur bike—replace the links in question or the entire chain.

REPLACE CHAIN

This work is required if the old chain is worn or in order to clean the existing chain. The description is based on a derailleur bike, while notes at the end of the description explain what to consider on a bike without derailleurs. As for which chain to choose, that depends on the cogs on the back: consult with a bike shop to make sure you get a chain suitable for the combination of cogs on your bike.

TOOLS & EQUIPMENT:

- chain rivet tool
- cloths

REMOVAL PROCEDURE:

1. While turning the cranks, with the rear wheel lifted off the ground, select the gear in which the chain runs over the

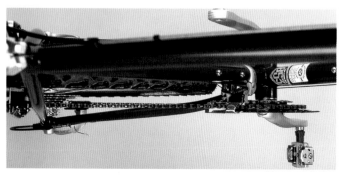

Above: Fig. 13.4. Chain lubrication.

Left: Fig. 13.3. Chain line.

Right: Fig. 13.5. Chain cleaning and lubrication with special tool.

smallest cog in the rear and the smallest chainring in the front.

2. Turn back the handle of the chain rivet tool (counterclockwise), so the pin of the tool is retracted all the way. Then place the tool between two links, with the pin of the tool firmly up against the chain link pin.

3. Turn the handle in (clockwise) firmly, pushing the chain link pin out; but don't push the pin out all the way (it will be practically impossible to replace the pin if you push it out all the way)—just far enough so no more than $1/32$ inch (about 0.5 mm) of the pin stays engaged.

4. Turn the handle back (counterclockwise) until it comes free of the chain, and remove the tool.

5. Twist the chain links apart at the point of the retracted chain link pin.

INSTALLATION PROCEDURE:

1. Select the gear by which the chain engages the smallest cog in the back and the smallest chainring in the front.

2. Working from the chain end that does not have the pin sticking out, guide the chain through the front derailleur cage, wrap it around the chainring, around the small rear cog, and over and between the derailleur pulleys as shown in Fig. 9.10 on page 72, until the two ends of the chain can be connected.

3. Place the slight inward protrusion of the pin that was pushed out over the inner link that forms the other end of the chain, and hold the two parts in place correctly aligned.

4. Turn the handle of the chain tool back far enough for the pin on the tool to clear the protruding end of the pin on the chain, and then turn it in

until there is firm contact between the two pins.

5. While continuing to hold the two chain links properly aligned, turn the handle of the chain tool in, pushing the chain link pin in all the way until it protrudes equally far on both sides; then remove the tool.

6. Apply sideways force, twisting in both directions, until the two chain links around the newly replaced pin rotate freely. If it can't be done this way, put the chain tool on from the opposite side and push the chain link pin back in slightly.

• On relatively wide chains (i.e. those not intended for use with 8-, 9-, and 10-speed cassettes), the connection can usually be loosened by using the chain tool in its second position, which pushes the links apart.

NOTE:

If the pin is accidentally pushed all the way out during disassembly, you can remove the last two links and replace them with a new two-link section of chain—taking care not to lose the pin again.

Left: Fig. 13.6. Pushing out the pin.

Above: Fig. 13.7. Hyperglide tool use.

Right: Fig. 13.8. Pushing the pin back in.

HYPERGLIDE NOTE:

On Shimano's Hyperglide chains, there is one slightly bigger link with a black finish (compared to the shiny bright appearance of the rest of the chain). That's the only pin to disconnect and connect the chain (of course, to shorten the chain, you'll break it at a different link, but you'll still connect at the black pin). That pin has to be discarded when removed and replaced by a new one, which has an extension that has to be cut off after installation.

- Use Shimano's special tool for working on Hyperglide chains, and keep a couple of spare black pins around.

CHAIN LENGTH

On a derailleur bike, the chain should be just long enough to wrap around the biggest chainring and the biggest cog while still leaving enough spring tension at the derailleur—and short enough not to hang loose while it runs over the smallest cog and the smallest chainring. If that can't be achieved, you need a rear derailleur on which the pulleys are farther apart, known as a wide-range or long-cage derailleur.

On a non-derailleur bike, the chain length should be such that there is about 2 cm (¾ in.) up-and-down movement possible in the middle of the free chain between cog and chainring. You can make minor adjustments by moving the rear wheel back or forth a little and clamping it in properly. On a wheel with a hub brake, this also requires you to loosen the counter-lever and re-tighten it in the right position once the wheel bolts are tightened.

Major corrections of the chain length (for derailleur and non-derailleur bikes alike) are made by removing or adding a section of chain consisting of an even number of links. Follow essentially the same procedure described above for chain removal and installation.

CHAINS WITH A MASTER LINK

The wider chain used on many non-derailleur bicycles can be

opened up and connected by means of the special so-called master link provided with these chains. It is built up as shown in Fig. 13.11. Remove it by prying off the spring clip with e.g. a small screwdriver (covering it with a cloth, so you don't lose the small spring). Then the loose link plate can be lifted off and the rest of the link (the fixed link plate with the two pins attached) comes out from the other side of the chain. When installing a master link, make sure the direction of rotation of the chain is such that the closed end of the spring clip points forward in the direction of chain rotation.

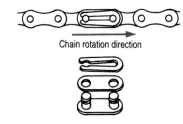

Chain rotation direction

Fig. 13.11. Master link installation diagram.

Above: Fig. 13.10. Breaking Hyperglide pin.

Left: Fig. 13.9. Twisting the chain to clear the pin.

Bottom right: Fig. 13.12. Damaged chain link.

14
PEDAL MAINTENANCE

Pedals come in two basic types—conventional and clipless. Conventional pedals can be used with regular footwear, while clipless pedals require special shoes equipped with matching engagement plates.

PEDAL BEARING TYPES

They also come with one of two bearing types: cartridge or cup-and-cone bearings. You can tell them apart as follows: If there's a removable dust cap on the outside end of the pedal, it's probably a conventional (adjustable) type; if not, it's definitely a cartridge-bearing type. Clipless pedals always have cartridge

bearings, while conventional pedals may be of either type.

Actually, there's a third bearing type too: sleeve bearings, as found on really cheap bikes; the only advice on those is to replace them with better pedals running on ball bearings.

Whatever type, the pedals are screwed into threaded holes at the end of the cranks. The left-side pedal has left-hand screw thread (and is usually marked with an "L"), while the right-side pedal has regular right-hand screw thread. If you're having difficulty tightening or loosening a pedal, first check whether you're turning them the right way or not—left-hand thread means tighten counter-clockwise and loosen clockwise.

Pedal adjustment or overhauling will be called for if the pedal either feels loose or does not turn freely. If it wobbles, there's a more serious problem: the axle, or spindle, is bent. In that case,

Above: Fig. 14.2. Clipless pedal.

Left: Fig. 14.1. Conventional pedal.

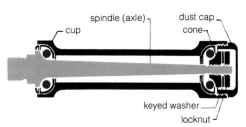

spindle (axle) · dust cap · cup · cone · keyed washer · locknut

Fig. 14.3. Cross-section of adjustable bearing pedal.

replace either the pedal axle (if available) or the whole pedal.

The release force of clipless pedals can be adjusted to suit your needs. If you use conventional pedals, you may want to use them in conjunction with "old-fashioned" toe-clips. Check and tighten their attachment screws to the front of the pedal occasionally to stop them from coming loose.

The other items you'll often find on a conventional pedal are little reflectors. Also check and tighten their attachments from time to time, and replace them if missing or broken.

With all pedal work, you should work on only one at a time. That's because some identical-looking parts of the two pedals are actually not identical and you would do serious damage if you mixed them up.

left-hand thread   right-hand thread
left-side pedal   right-side pedal

Fig. 14.4. Pedal screw thread for left- and right-side pedals.

REPLACE PEDALS

This work can be called for if the pedal is damaged—or when the bike has to be stored in a small box, e.g. to be transported. Note that the pedal wrench used for this work may either be the metric size 15 mm or the non-metric size $^9/_{16}$ inch.

TOOLS & EQUIPMENT:

- pedal wrench (or, if not too tight, a (preferably long) 6 mm Allen wrench)

- lubricant

- cloth

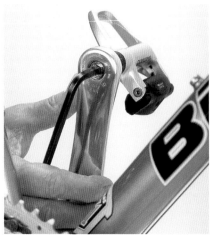

Above: Fig. 14.6. Removing pedal using Allen wrench.

Left: Fig. 14.5. Removing pedal using pedal wrench.

Top right: Fig. 14.7. Pedal removed from the crank.

Bottom right: Fig. 14.8. Lubricating the pedal thread before installing the pedal.

REMOVAL PROCEDURE:

1. Place the pedal wrench on the flat surfaces of the stub between the pedal and the crank. (If the pedal is not on too tight, it can usually be done with the Allen wrench, reaching the hexagonal recess that's present in the end of most modern pedals from the back of the crank.)

2. Hold the crank arm firmly and:

    • for the right-side pedal, turn counterclockwise to loosen;

    • for the left-side pedal, turn clockwise.

3. Unscrew the pedal all the way.

INSTALLATION PROCEDURE:

1 Clean the thread surfaces in the cranks and on the pedals, and apply some lubricant.

2. Carefully align the thread of the pedal stub with the thread in the crank and start screwing it in by hand (counterclockwise for the left-side pedal).

3. Screw in the pedal fully with the pedal wrench (or from the back of the crank, using the Allen wrench). There's no need to tighten them excessively, because the pedaling motion will tighten them further.

ADJUST RELEASE FORCE OF CLIPLESS PEDAL

If it is too hard to get your foot out of a clipless pedal, or if it does not hold the shoe firmly enough, you can adjust the spring tension.

TOOLS & EQUIPMENT:

- Allen wrench to fit the adjustment bolt(s)

PROCEDURE

1. Locate the tension adjustment bolt or bolts on the pedal in question.

2. Tighten or loosen the bolt(s) as required.

3. Check operation and fine-tune adjustment if necessary.

ADJUST CONVENTIONAL PEDAL BEARINGS

This work can usually be done with the pedal still attached to the bike. However, if the pedal has a cage that wraps around, it may be necessary to remove the cage to gain access to the outboard bearing.

TOOLS & EQUIPMENT:

- tool to remove dust cap

- open-ended wrench and/or socket wrench

- small screwdriver

PROCEDURE:

1. Holding the pedal at the crank, loosen the dust cap (it's usually threaded but may be snapped on, in which case you'll have to pry it off).

2. Unscrew the locknut by about one turn, and lift the keyed washer.

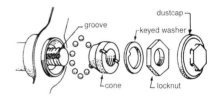

Fig. 14.11. Conventional pedal bearing adjustment detail.

Above: Fig. 14.10. Adjusting release force on clipless road bike pedal.

Left: Fig. 14.9. Adjusting release force on Shimano SPD mountain bike pedal.

Right: Fig. 14.12. Parts of an adjustable-bearing pedal.

3. Using whatever tool fits the cone (the small screwdriver if the top of the cone is slotted), turn the cone in or out by about ¼ turn to tighten or loosen the bearing respectively.

4. Holding the cone with the screwdriver, tighten the locknut.

5. Check the adjustment of the bearing and fine-tune the adjustment if necessary, making sure the locknut is firmed up properly.

6. Reinstall the dust cap.

LUBRICATE & OVERHAUL CONVENTIONAL PEDAL

Although this work can be done with the pedal still on the bike, it's recommended to remove it first—and reinstall it afterward. As mentioned in the adjusting procedure, you may have to remove the cage to lubricate the outboard bearing.

Because some pedal parts are not interchangeable between left and right, you should keep all the parts separate or work on only one pedal at a time.

TOOLS & EQUIPMENT:

- tool to remove dust cap

- open-ended wrench and/or socket wrench

- small screwdriver

- cloth

- bearing grease

DISASSEMBLY PROCEDURE:

1. Holding the pedal at the crank, loosen the dust cap (it's usually threaded, but may be snapped on, in which case you'll be able to pry it off).

2. Unscrew the locknut and remove it; then also remove the keyed washer.

3. Using whatever tool fits the cone (the small screwdriver if the top of the cone is slotted), unscrew and remove the cone.

4. Pull the pedal body and the pedal axle apart, catching all the bearing balls with the cloth.

OVERHAULING AND REASSEMBLY PROCEDURE:

1. Clean and inspect all parts, replacing any that are pitted, corroded, or otherwise damaged. It's always a good idea

Above: Fig. 14.15. Lubricated bearing cup and bearing balls exposed.

Top left: Fig. 14.13. Dustcap removed, showing bearing with locknut.

Bottom left: Fig. 14.14. Locknut and keyed washer removed, showing adjustable cup.

Right: Fig. 14.16. Replacing the cage of a conventional pedal.

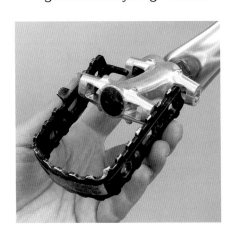

to replace the bearing balls, which on pedals are not held in a retainer.

2. Fill both bearing cups with bearing grease, and push the bearing balls in.

3. Slide the pedal body back over the axle, with the larger bearing cup toward the crank; be careful not to push the bearing balls out.

4. Install the cone until the bearing feels just barely loose.

5. Install the keyed washer with the tab matching the groove (replace it if it is worn so much that it can slip out of the groove).

6. Install the locknut and tighten it against the cone.

7. Check the bearing adjustment and fine-tune it if necessary.

8. Install the dust cap.

MAINTENANCE OF CARTRIDGE-BEARING PEDAL

You can do this work either with the pedal still installed on the bike or removed. Because some pedal parts are not interchangeable between left and right, you should keep all the parts separate or work on only one pedal at a time.

TOOLS & EQUIPMENT:

• wrench to fit the flat hexagonal stub that screws into the pedal body

• cloth

• lubricant

DISASSEMBLY PROCEDURE

1. Holding the hexagonal stub that's screwed into the back of the pedal body with the wrench, unscrew the pedal

Above: Fig. 14.18. Cartridge-bearing pedal disassembled.

Left: Fig. 14.17. Removing cartridge from pedal housing.

Right: Fig. 14.19. Shoe-plate installation or adjustment.

body off by hand. (It may have either right- or left-hand screw thread.)

2. Pull off the pedal body. You have now separated the pedal axle with one (inner) bearing from the pedal body with the other (outer) bearing.

3. Check to see whether there is access to the pedal body that allows you to remove the outer bearing—and do so if you can (otherwise, a special tool will be needed, and you should leave this job to a bike shop mechanic).

OVERHAULING AND ASSEMBLY PROCEDURE:

1. Check the condition of any parts you can see. If the axle is bent, replace the entire cartridge (if available—if not, you'll have to replace the pedals).

2. If you can remove the bearings, do so. If not, try to lift the bearing seals to gain access to them.

3. Lubricate the bearings and re-install the parts on the axle.

4. Reinstall any parts you removed and reinsert the cartridge into the pedal body.

5. Screw the cartridge in all the way.

INSTALL & ADJUST SHOE PLATES

Clipless pedals, must be used with special matching shoe plates, or cleats. Follow this procedure to adjust them properly.

TOOLS & EQUIPMENT:

• 5 mm Allen wrench

ADJUSTING PROCEDURE:

1. Wearing the shoe, establish the center of the ball of the foot and mark it with a line with a felt-tip pen on the side of the sole.

2. Take off the shoe and loosen the Allen bolts that hold the cleat to the shoe by about one turn—just enough to force the cleat's position by hand, but not loose.

3. Place the shoe on the pedal with the cleat engaged in the clip of the pedal, and check

the location of the line relative to the center of the pedal. Shift the shoe plate relative to the shoe until it is above the center of the pedal, keeping the shoe parallel to the crank.

4. Tighten the bolts and test ride the bike. If you detect sideways angular movement in the knee, you have to fine-tune the adjustment to shift the heel of the shoe in or out a little. Repeat until comfortable.

CONVERTIBLE PEDALS

Some pedals have a clipless mechanism, combined with a platform for use with normal shoes.

To get the benefit of the clipless mechanism, you can re-

Above: Fig. 14.20. Removing shoe platform from a convertible pedal.

Right: Fig. 14.21. How to route the toe strap on a pedal with toe-clips.

move the outer part. First release the spring tension of the clipless mechanism, then use a small screwdriver to pry the platform out of the clamp of the clipless mechanism.

TOE-CLIPS

Except rubber-block pedals found on city cruisers, most conventional pedals lend themselves to the installation of toe-clips, which gives the same advantage as clipless pedals without the need for special shoes.

Use a screwdriver and a small wrench to install the clips. Then thread the strap through with the buckle on the outside of the pedal, and twisting it as shown in Fig. 14.21.

You may be able to install a pedal reflector on both ends of the pedal (using its screws to hold down the toe-clip in the front.

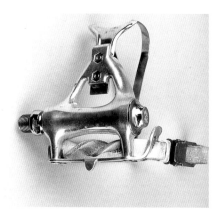

15 RIM BRAKE MAINTENANCE

M ost modern bicycles are equipped with one of two versions of the rim brake: mountain bikes usually come with so-called V-brakes, while road bikes are usually equipped with double-pivot sidepull brakes.

TYPES OF BRAKES

In addition to rim brakes, which are covered in this chapter, there are also disk brakes and various types of hub brakes. The former are the subject of Chapter 16, while the latter are covered in Chapter 17.

In addition to V-brakes and sidepull brakes, there are still some other rim brakes around, especially on older bikes. These include cantilever brakes for mountain bikes and touring bikes, and conventional sidepull and centerpull brakes for road bikes.

The principle of operation of all rim brakes is that two brake pads, made of a high-friction compound and usually connected to the brake arms by means of metal holders, are pressed inward against the sides

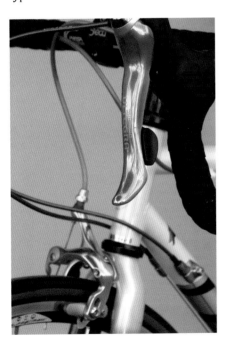

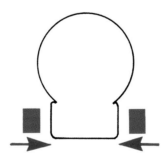

Fig. 15.2. Caliper rim brake principle.

Left: Fig. 15.1. Typical rim brake system: brake lever and calipers, connected by a cable.

Right: Fig. 15.3. V-brake, as found on most mountain bikes and other flat-handlebar machines.

of the wheel rim. To achieve that, the rider compresses a lever that is mounted on the handlebars, which is connected to the brake mechanism via a flexible cable.

THE V-BRAKE

The V-brake, also referred to as "direct-pull" or "linear-pull" brake, is most commonly installed on mountain bikes, city bikes, and hybrids. It consists of two brake arms that pivot around bosses installed directly on the fork and the seatstays. The inner and outer ca-

bles pull the upper ends of the brake arms together and the brake pads are attached to the brake arms halfway between the pivot and the cable attachment point.

The inner cable is clamped directly to one brake arm, while the outer cable ends in a bent tubular piece (referred to as a "noodle") that sits in a clamp attached to the other brake arm. This is the point to undo when you have to release the cable tension.

brake arms take care of the movement of the brake arms relative to each other. The latter type is the one referred to as double-pivot sidepull brake. The brake pads are held at the lower points of the brake arms, and the inner and outer cable are attached to extensions of the two brake arms that stick out to one side. A quick-release mechanism and a cable adjuster are attached to the brake arm extension that holds the outer cable.

THE SIDEPULL BRAKE

The sidepull brake (whether it's the now common double-pivot type or not) is used on most road bikes. It comprises a separate unit mounted by means of a single attachment bolt installed in a hole in the middle of the fork crown or the rear brake bridge (a tubular piece connecting the seatstays).

Either the central bolt or two different pivots on one of the

THE CANTILEVER BRAKE

Cantilever brakes are still the best choice for tandems and touring bikes. Like the V-brake, they are mounted on bosses welded on the fork blades and the seatstays. The brake arms of the cantilever brake stick out more to the sides.

Instead of the direct attachment of the cable to the top of the brake arms, the two brake arms, which are much shorter than they are on the V-brake, are connected by means of a straddle cable, which in turn is con-

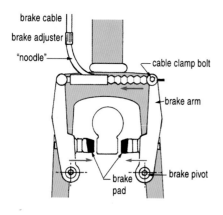

Fig. 15.4. Principle of the V-brake.

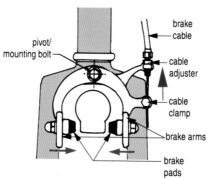

Fig. 15.6 Principle of the sidepull brake.

Left: Fig. 15.5. Double-pivot sidepull brake, as used on most modern road bikes.

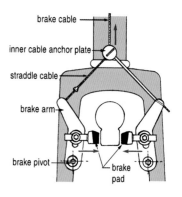

Fig. 15.7. Principle of the cantilever brake.

nected in the middle to the actual brake cable. The outer cable is held at a cable anchor attached to the frame some distance above the brake arms.

THE CENTERPULL BRAKE

This type of brake is hardly used on new bikes, but it's still around on older machines. It works on the same principle as the cantilever brake, complete with straddle cable. The only difference is the fact that the brake is a single unit with the brake arms mounted on a yoke holding the pivot and

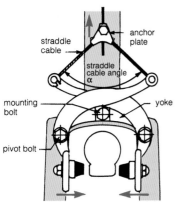

Fig. 15.9. Principle of centerpull brake.

mounting bolts. The yoke is mounted to the fork or the frame by means of a central mounting bolt. Both sidepull and centerpull brakes are also referred to as caliper brakes.

COMMON RIM BRAKE FEATURES

There are a couple of aspects that all rim brakes have in common, and these are the first, and most general, points to pay attention to when checking or maintaining the brakes.

Adjustability is usually provided either at the point where the cable comes out of the lever or at the point where the cable connects to the brake mechanism. Somewhere in the system is usually a quick-release device or some easily handled method of unhooking the inner or outer cable.

The most common adjustments are those of the brake pad position relative to the rim and

Above: Fig. 15.10. Centerpull brake.

Top left: Fig. 15.8. Cantilever brake.

the cable tension. The former adjustment assures that the brake pads wear evenly and work fully when engaged; the latter adjustment determines how quickly and consequently, how powerfully they can be engaged.

When working on the brakes, be aware that they should be treated as complete systems, which includes not only the brakes themselves, but also the brake levers, the control cables, and any attachments through which the cables run. In fact, even the condition of the rim and the spokes can influence brake performance.

BRAKE TEST

To carry out the brake test suggested for the monthly inspection—or whenever you feel the need to verify the brakes work properly, such as before a long tour—proceed as follows:

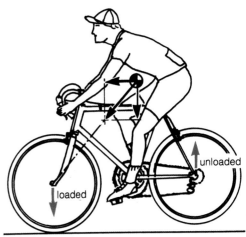

Fig. 15.11. Reaction to brake application.

TOOLS & EQUIPMENT:

- Usually none required, but please wear a helmet.

PROCEDURE:

1. Check to make sure the rims are clean, and if not, clean it with a slightly abrasive pad and water or mild solvent, followed by a dry cloth.

2. Check to make sure the brake pads are not excessively or irregularly worn, and replace them if they are.

3. Make sure the brakes themselves are firmly attached to the bike, the brake cable is firmly anchored and does not have any kinks, broken or frayed strands, and that the brake levers are firmly attached to the handlebars and can be easily reached.

4. For each brake (front and rear), check to make sure the brake pads touch the wheel rim parallel with the rim and with 1–2 mm clearance between the top of the brake

pad and the edge of the rim. If not, make corrections as described under *Brake Adjustments* on page 109.

5. Check to make sure the brake pads touch the rim firmly when you depress the brake lever to within ¾ inch (2 cm) from the handlebars.

6. Get on the bike and ride it at a brisk walking speed (about 3–4 mph, or 5–7 km/h) on a clear, level paved surface, such as an empty parking lot. When doing the actual test, you must be going in a straight line.

FRONT BRAKE TEST PROCEDURE:

1. To test the front brake, apply the left-side brake lever, gradually increasing hand force. If the bike starts to tip forward (i.e. the rear end of the bike starts lifting off the ground)

once the brake is fully applied, the brake force is adequate. Immediately let go of the brake to prevent falling.

- If you can't get this to happen, the brake is not effective enough. Follow the procedure below to adjust the brake.

- If the bike starts to tip forward almost immediately, the brake is grabbing too vigorously for sensitively controlled braking. Follow the procedures below to adjust the brake.

- If the bike, or just the brake, vibrates, rumbles, or squeals when you apply the brake, it also needs attention.

- If applying the brake seems to require excessive force at the lever, there may be a problem with either the cable or the levers.

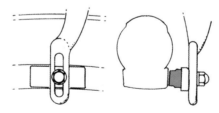

Fig. 15.12. Correct brake pad position relative to the rim.

Left: Fig. 15.13. Adjusting brake pad on a sidepull brake.

Right: Fig. 15.14. Adjusting brake pad on a cantilever brake.

REAR BRAKE TEST PROCEDURE:

Proceed just as described above for the front brake test. However, the action will be different: the rear wheel should start skidding when the brake lever is pulled beyond ¾ inch (20 mm) from the handlebars, and it should be possible to apply the brake gradually before reaching that point.

BRAKE ADJUSTMENTS

The following sections contain summaries of the various procedures to improve the performance of the brake when the brake test has revealed that something's not working quite right.

ADJUST BRAKE APPLICATION

Over time, brake pad wear, cable stretch, and pivot bushing wear in

the various components combine to make the point where the brake lever activates the brake to get closer and closer to the point where the lever gets too close to the handlebars to apply sufficient force. It must be readjusted if it no longer applies powerful enough braking force when it is ¾ inch (2 cm) from the handlebars.

TOOLS & EQUIPMENT:

• Usually none required, sometimes a wrench for the cable clamp bolt at the brake.

PROCEDURE:

1. Find the adjuster for your particular brake. On road bikes with sidepull brakes, it's usually on the brake arm to which the outer cable is anchored.

Left: Fig. 15.15. Adjusting cable tension on a sidepull brake.

Above: Fig. 15.16. Use of the brake quick-release on a sidepull brake, shown here while tightening.

On mountain bike brakes, it's usually on the brake lever at the point where the outer cable comes out of the lever body.

• Establish what kind of adjuster it is. On most modern road bikes, it's the type without a locknut. On older bikes it may be the type with a locknut.

2. Also find the cable quick-release, which on most road bike brakes is on the brake arm where the inner cable is clamped in. On V-brakes, it's the bent piece of metal tubing that guides the outer cable between the brake arms—to use it, squeeze the brake arms together at the top and wiggle that tube out from the bracket that holds it at the bottom.

3. Depending on the type of adjuster:

• If you're working on a bike with the adjuster without locknut, first use the quick-release to untension the cable.

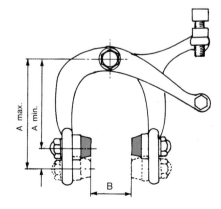

Fig. 15.17. Brake reach diagram.

Then turn the adjuster in about one turn (to tighten) or out (in case you want the brake to grab later than it does now). Then tighten the quick-release again, check and repeat if necessary.

PROCEDURE FOR OLDER BIKES:

If the brake has an adjuster with a locknut (usually the case on older bikes), proceed as follows:

1. Loosen the locknut by several turns, which can usually be done by hand, without the need for a tool.

2. Turn the adjusting barrel relative to the part into which it is screwed (to loosen) or out (to tighten) the tension on the cable. Loosening will open up the brake; tightening will do the opposite.

3. Holding the adjusting barrel with one hand, tighten the locknut again, then check and repeat if necessary.

CABLE CLAMPING ADJUSTING PROCEDURE:

If you run out of adjusting range, the cable has to be clamped in at a different point:

1. Release the cable tension with the quick-release (or unhook the cable) and then loosen the adjuster as far as possible (after unscrewing the locknut, if present).

2. Loosen the bolt or the nut that clamps the end of the inner cable at one of the brake arms (or, in the case of cantilever and centerpull brakes, the particular location where

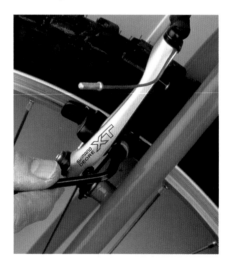

the main cable ends) by about one full turn.

3. With the needle-nose pliers, pull the cable about 3/8 inch (1 cm) further in and tighten the bolt or the nut again.

4. Tighten the adjuster (and the locknut, if provided) about 1/4 of the way, then tighten the quick-release and check operation of the brake, and readjust if necessary.

ADJUST BRAKE PADS

Make this correction if the brake test or any other inspection revealed that the brake pads do not lie flat and straight on the side of the rim with about $1/16$ inch (1–2 mm) clearance to the tire when the brake lever is pulled in.

TOOLS & EQUIPMENT:

- matching wrenches

PROCEDURE:

1. Holding the brake pad with one hand, undo the bolt or

Above: Fig. 15.19. Adjusting brake pad on a V-brake.

Left: Fig. 15.18. Adjusting brake at the brake lever of a flat-handlebar bike.

Right: Fig. 15.20. Adjusting brake pad on a sidepull brake.

the nut that holds it to the brake arm by about one turn—just enough to allow controlled movement into the right position.

2. While applying the brake lever so the brake pad is pushed up against the rim, twist the brake pad into the appropriate orientation and hold it firmly in place there.

3. While holding the brake pad firmly, let go of the brake lever (unless you have an assistant to do that for you) use the free hand to tighten the bolt or the nut that holds the brake pad to the brake arm.

4. Check to make sure both brake pads are properly aligned; make any corrections necessary, then re-tighten.

TOEING IN NOTE:

Preferably, the front end (the "trailing edge") of the brake pads should touch the rim first, with the whole pad settling when more force is applied. This is achieved

by a procedure called "toeing in," described under *Brake Squeal Compensation*.

BRAKE CENTERING

This work is required if one brake pad touches the rim before the other one, especially if it rubs on the surface of the rim while riding.

Depending on the type of brake, you may be able to find one or more small grub screws that point in vertically from the top (on a dual-pivot sidepull brake) or sideways at the pivots. Check what happens if you tighten or loosen these screws. Adjust these screws until the brake works symmetrically, if possible. Then make sure the brake is still working properly in other ways and make any final adjustments that may be needed.

If there is no such screw, or if the desired result cannot be obtained, you may have to rotate the entire brake a little (usually the case on older caliper brakes). Do that either with a small thin wrench that fits two flat surfaces on the mounting bolt on many sidepull brakes. Otherwise, undo the mounting bolt, realign the entire brake and hold it steady there, applying force at the lever; then tighten the mounting bolt again.

Left: Fig. 15.21. Centering a double-pivot sidepull brake.

Right: Fig. 15.22. V-brakes and cantilever brakes can be centered by choosing a different hole to insert the spring for one or both brake arms.

On V-brakes and cantilever brakes, the asymmetrical action may be due to uneven spring tension at the brake arms. To correct that, remove the brake arms, as described under *Overhaul Brake* on page 115, and either hook one or both of the springs into a different hole on the mounting plate (if provided) on the pivot boss, or use pliers to tension one of the springs more. Then reassemble the brake arms, check operation of the brake, and make any other adjustments that may be needed.

BRAKE SQUEAL COMPENSATION

Sometimes, brakes seem to work alright but make a squealing noise when applied. You may have to just live with it, but it's worthwhile checking whether it can be eliminated first. That's probably possible if your brake pads are mounted with some intermediate parts between the brake arm and the pad itself. These allow you to rotate the pad in another direction as well as around the mounting bolt.

If the brake pads can be rotated in the other plane, adjust the pad so that the front of the pad touches the rim when there is still 2 mm (³/₃₂ inch) of "air" between the pad and the rim in the back. This condition is referred to as "toed in." If this does not do the trick, also try it the other way round, the back touching the rim first (which you might call "toed out"). If still no luck, you'd probably best put it back in the position where the whole pad touches the rim at the same time.

BRAKE RUMBLE COMPENSATION

If the brake rumbles, and perhaps the whole bike vibrates, when you apply the brake, it may be a matter of a dirty wheel rim, on which the brake pad does not have a good continuous contact when you apply the brake. So check that first and clean and dry the side of the rims thoroughly.

If this does not solve the problem, it's usually because something is loose somewhere

on your bike, and you'd better tighten it. First suspect is the brake itself. Check the mounting bolts of the brakes and the individual brake arms and all related pivot points. However, sometimes it's another part of the bike that's loose — most typically the headset, for which you are referred to Chapter 19.

REPLACE BRAKE CABLE

If operating the brake seems to require excessive force despite poor braking, the problem is probably due to the cable. It may be kinked, dirty or corroded, or there may be broken strands. Inspect the cable for obvious signs of damage. Replace it if the problem is not alleviated by cleaning and lubrication. Buy a replacement cable of at least the same

Above: Fig. 15.24. Releasing or installing cantilever straddle cable.

Left: Fig. 15.23. Releasing or installing V-brake outer cable from its anchor.

Right: Fig. 15.25. Unhooking cantilever outer cable from its anchor.

length, making sure it has the same type of nipple at the end where it is hooked into the brake lever.

TOOLS & EQUIPMENT:

*   wrench for inner cable clamp bolt at brake

*   needle-nose pliers

*   lubricant

*   cloth

*   cable cutters or diagonal cutters

PROCEDURE:

1. Undo the bolt or the nut that clamps in the cable at the brake.

2. Pull the brake lever and hold the brake calliper pushed against the rim; then release the lever, thus loosening the cable tension. For aero-brake levers (with hidden cable), use the needle-nose pliers to grab the end of the cable near the nipple inside the brake lever, and pull enough cable free to get at it by hand to remove

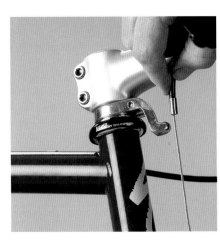

the rest of the inner cable. Also catch any sections of outer cable that were used and any ferrules that went around the end of the outer cable where it was held at anchor points.

• On mountain bike brake levers, the brake cable can usually be lifted out easily once you turn the adjuster and the locknut into such an orientation that the grooves that are cut into both parts line up with a cutout in the brake mounting bracket.

• On road bikes, if there seems to be a kink in a section of outer cable that lies under

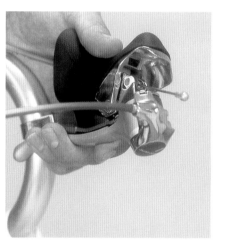

the handlebar tape, remove the handlebar tape, replace that piece of outer cable and re-wrap the handlebars as described in Chapter 18.

3. Using a grease- or wax-soaked cloth, apply some lubricant to the new inner cable before installing it.

4. Depress the brake lever and find the place where the cable nipple is held, then insert the cable. You may need to wiggle and twist the innards of the lever a little at the point where the nipple is held.

• On mountain bike brake levers, the brake cable can usually be installed at the lever by turning the adjuster and the

Above: Fig. 15.28. Removing cable from lever.

Top left: Fig. 15.26. Brake cable released from integrated brake-shifter lever.

Bottom left: Fig. 15.27. Turning cable adjuster to allow cable to be removed at mountain bike lever.

Right: Fig. 15.29. Attaching V-brake cable while holding it taut with pliers.

locknut into such an orientation that the slots cut into both parts line up with the cutout in the brake mounting bracket.

5. Route the inner cable through the various sections of outer cable and cable stops (making sure to install the ferrules at the points where the outer cable ends at the cable stops, the brake, and the lever).

6. Clamp the end of the inner cable in at the termination point on the brake while pulling it taut with the needle-nose pliers.

7. Provisionally adjust the brake tension. Then test the brake operation, and make any final adjustments in accordance with the procedure *Brake Adjustments*.

REPLACE BRAKE LEVERS

That's probably only necessary if you've had an accident with the

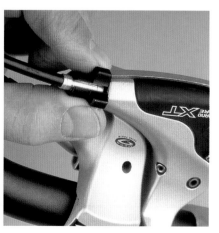

bike. On modern road bikes, that can be quite expensive and complex, since on these machines the brake lever is integrated with the gear shifter, making for one complex and expensive item, which affects the gearing as well. This description ignores the gearing aspect of such a job, concentrating only on the brake function of the lever. (Refer to Chapter 9 for information on work involving the gear shifting function, if that is pertinent.) Before removing the brake lever, you'll have to remove the handlebar tape and the bar-end cap on a road bike or sometimes the handgrip on other bike types.

TOOLS & EQUIPMENT:

- wrench for lever mounting bolt

- needle-nose pliers

- wrench for brake cable clamp bolt (at the brake)

PROCEDURE:

1. Remove the brake cable, following the procedure *Replace Brake Cable* on page 112.

2. Locate the mounting bolt. If it's not externally visible, it will be accessed either from inside when you depress the brake lever (on conventional brake levers) or from under the rubber brake hood (on integrated brake/shift levers). Loosen the bolt far enough to wiggle the lever off to the end of the handlebars.

3. Loosen the bolt on the replacement lever just far enough to allow it to slide over the handlebars. Avoid taking it out all the way, because it can be very hard to get the various parts of the mounting clamp together once the bolt is out.

4. Slide the lever into position and orient it so that it can be

Above: Fig. 15.31. Cable end protector.

Left: Fig. 15.30. Cutting inner cable.

Top right: Fig. 15.32. Removing or installing road bike lever.

Bottom right: Fig. 15.33. Special lever with la latch to use as "drag brake" when riding downhill.

comfortably reached while riding the bike. If necessary, use the lever on the opposite side of the handlebars as a guide regarding mounting position and angle.

5. Tighten the mounting bolt fully, making sure the lever stays in the correct position and orientation.

6. Reinstall the cable as described under *Replace Brake Cable*, and test operation of the brake, making any adjustments that may be necessary.

OVERHAUL BRAKE

This work differs according to the type of brake that's installed on the bike—whether it's a caliper brake (which comes off in one piece) or a mountain bike brake (on which the brake arms are mounted on pivot bosses attached to the frame or the fork).

1. Either way, first untension the quick-release or unhook the cable at the brake.

2. Depending on the type of brake:

    • If it's a V-brake or a cantilever brake, remove the brake cable clamping bolt.

    • If it's a caliper brake, first undo the brake cable, then remove the mounting bolt with which the entire brake is held on the bike.

3. Remove the bolts with which the brake arms are installed on their pivots, then also remove the brake pads from the brake arms.

4. Remove all other components (including springs, bushings, and washers).

5. Clean and inspect the condition of all parts and replace anything damaged.

6. Slightly lubricate all parts and apply wax to the exterior surfaces, then reassemble all parts on the brake assembly (on caliper brakes) or the pivots (on V-brakes or cantilever brakes).

    • On some cantilever brakes and V-brakes, there is a choice of three holes to insert the end of the spring at each pivot, depending on the spring tension. First choose the middle hole; if after assembly the brake turns out not to be centered and no amount of adjusting will cure it, undo the brake pivot bolt again, insert the spring in one of the other holes (depending on whether this was the one

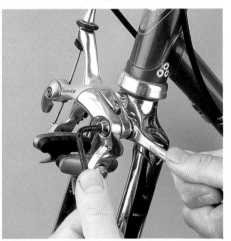

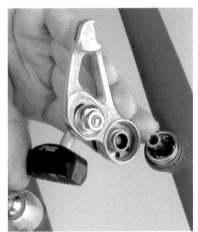

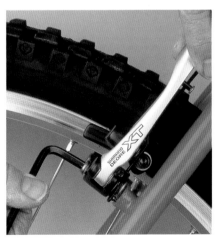

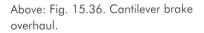

Above: Fig. 15.36. Cantilever brake overhaul.

Top left: Fig. 15.34. Dual-pivot sidepull brake overhaul.

Bottom left: Fig. 15.35. V-brake overhaul.

Top right: Fig. 15.37. Sidepull brake installation.

Bottom right: Fig. 15.38. Brake shoe installation.

with too much or the one with too little tension), and reinstall the brake arm.

7. Reattach the cable and adjust it loosely, then tension the quick-release (caliper brake) or attach the outer cable (V-brake or cantilever brake.

8. Test operation of the brake and make any adjustments necessary.

STIRRUP BRAKES

Still used on heavy-duty roadsters, this type of brake is operated via a system of pull rods and pivots that connect the brake levers with the brake units. They work by pulling the brake pads outward against the inside of the rim.

By way of maintenance, clean and lubricate all pivot points occasionally. If they don't work well, it's usually a matter of adjusting, just like other rim brakes. However, sometimes one of the pull rods may be bent, and your brake will be fixed by straightening it.

HYDRAULIC BRAKES & THEIR CONTROLS

Rare enough not to discuss in great detail here, hydraulic rim brakes should at least be mentioned.

Instead of a cable, there's a hydraulic tube filled with a liquid that transfers the force from the

lever (which has a cylinder and a piston to compress the liquid as the lever is depressed) to the brake. Actually, this method is more common in the case of disk brakes than it is for rim brakes. Be careful not to pinch or damage the hydraulic tube.

Occasionally, when the brake begins to feel "mushy," you should bleed the system (i.e. let any air bubbles out of the tube). Since this type of application is more commonly encountered with disk brakes, their maintenance will be described in some detail in Chapter 16.

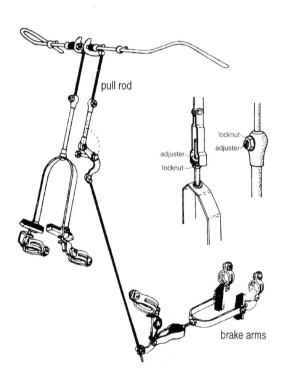

Fig. 15.39. Pull-rod-operated stirrup brake and adjusting details.

Fig. 15.40. Stirrup brake principle.

Right: Fig. 15.42. Hydraulic rim brake.

Below: Fig. 15.41. Hydraulic rim brake lever.

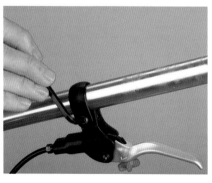

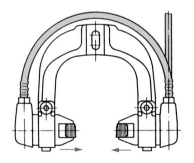

Fig. 15.43. Hydraulic rim brake diagram.

16
DISK BRAKE MAINTENANCE

First used only on downhill mountain bikes, disk brakes are now making inroads in the field of more common bike use. This chapter deals with their installation and basic maintenance, including the issues relating to hydraulic operation.

OPERATING PRINCIPLE

In essence, disk brakes work like regular rim brakes, except that they work on a flat circular disk attached to the wheel hub instead of the rim. A pair of brake pads is held in a set of calipers mounted on a frame tube, so that they can clamp down on the rotating disk to slow it down. The function of the counter-lever that's part of all other hub brakes, is taken over by a set of two attachment lugs that hold the brake caliper unit to the fork or the rear stays.

Operation of disk brakes can be either by means of cables like those used for rim brakes, or they may be hydraulically operated. In case of hydraulic operation, the brake lever incorporates a hydraulic oil reservoir, and there is another reservoir at the caliper unit. The two are connected by means of hydraulic tubing.

Modern disk brakes work great for mountain bike use.

Fig. 16.1. Disk brake diagram.

Above: Fig. 16.2. Typical hydraulic disk brake.

Right: Fig. 16.3. Cable-operated disk brake.

However, most models available to date can not handle the amount of heat generated in tandem use on long downhill sections, except as an auxiliary brake, relying mainly on conventional rim brakes.

DISK BRAKE TEST

To test whether a disk brake works properly, follow the same procedure as the one outlined for rim brakes in Chapter 15:

1. First check to make sure all components of the system (brake, lever, and tubing) are firmly attached and there's no sign of leakage of hydraulic liquid (or, in the case of cable-operation, no frayed or kinked cables.

2. Riding slowly, it should be possible to apply the front brake forcefully enough for the rear wheel to start lifting off the ground. Then immediately let go of that brake lever.

3. For the rear brake, it should be possible to make the wheel skid on smooth, dry pavement.

If the brake does not perform adequately, the most common cause is air in the hydraulic system. Follow the bleeding instructions given under *Hydraulic System Maintenance* to correct this problem.

Make sure the brake levers are mounted close enough to the center of the handlebars to allow you to grip the end of the lever. You can apply more force there.

DISK CHECK & MAINTENANCE

The brake disks are attached to special hubs by means of shal-

Above: Fig. 16.5. Adjusting cable-operated disk brake.

Left: Fig. 16.4. Tightening disk bolts using a Torx wrench.

Right: Fig. 16.6. Inserting protector between brake pads when disk is removed.

low-headed Allen bolts or Torx bolts (which have a star-shaped recess). Use a fitting wrench to make sure they are properly tightened.

Keep hydraulic liquid and other oils away from the disk, and clean any oil, dirt, or brake pad deposits with rubbing alcohol.

If the disk drags on the calipers, it's *not* corrected by anything you do to the disk but by moving the calipers in or out a little (see below).

DISK BRAKE CALIPER MAINTENANCE

The calipers are attached to standardized bosses attached to the frame at the rear dropout and to the back of the front fork. They're held in place with 6 mm Allen bolts, and they too must be kept firmly tightened.

Never apply the brake lever when the wheel (with the disk) is not in the bike. This would make the brake pads bind together, making it hard to separate them. Always insert the plastic protector

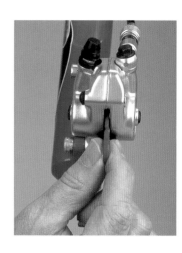

plate that comes with the brake unit when removing the wheel.

Clean the pads with a piece of emery cloth about once a month or whenever the brakes squeal.

The disk should run exactly in the middle between the brake pads. There are adjusting bolts on both sides of the calipers, which can be turned in or out to adjust the pad location until they are both equally far from the disk.

The mounting location of the calipers relative to the center of the wheel—and to the disk—is pretty much standardized. How-

ever, some disk brake manufacturers (most notably Hope) use their own non-standard mounting method. If necessary, you can add or remove shim washers to push the calipers further out.

HYDRAULIC SYSTEM MAINTENANCE

The following instructions apply to all hydraulic brakes— including caliper brakes. If the brakes feel "spongy," you'll have to bleed the system, i.e. let air bubbles out. At least once a year, you should flush all the oil out and replace it with fresh oil.

There are two different types of hydraulic liquid in use for hydraulic brakes: DOT No. 4 and hydraulic oil. Both are available in automotive supply stores more cheaply than in a bike shop (but be careful not to ruin the seals by using the wrong type for your particular brakes).

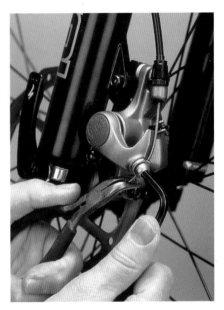

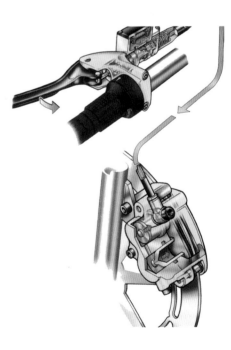

Above: Fig. 16.9. Installing brake on standard lugs using a mounting adapter.

Top left: Fig. 16.7. Installing a standard-mount brake caliper unit.

Bottom left: Fig. 16.8. Installing a Hayes-type brake on matching mounting lugs.

Top right: Fig. 16.10. Clamping in the cable at the brake caliper unit.

Fig. 16.11. Manufacturer's diagram showing hydraulic system (Magura).

TOOLS & EQUIPMENT:

- 12 in (30 cm) of 3/16 in. (5 mm) flexible plastic tubing

- small plastic syringe

- only if replenishing: hydraulic liquid of the specified type

- empty jam jar

- latex gloves for protection

- any tools required to open reservoir at brake lever

PROCEDURE

1. Clamp the bike in a work stand so that the bake lever is as high as possible and the brake unit as low as possible. Turn the brake lever so that the reservoir cover is horizontal.

2. Remove the screws to open up the reservoir at the brake lever.

3. Attach the tube to the bleed nipple at the brake unit, holding the tube pointing straight up, but curved down at the top to drain into the jam jar. Then open the bleed nipple about ¼ turn.

4. Fill the syringe with brake fluid and start filling it into the reservoir at the lever while gently pumping the lever repeatedly.

5. Watch the oil being pushed through the bleed tube and keep filling until no air bubbles come through.

6. Close the bleed nipple and the reservoir at the lever.

7. Test operation and repeat until the brake action is firm.

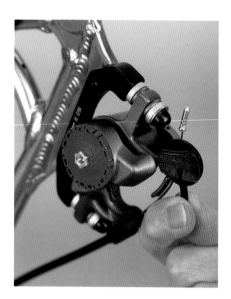

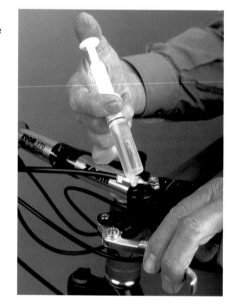

Top left: Fig. 16.12. Replacing the brake pads of a disk brake.

Bottom left: Fig. 16.13. Hydraulic tube connection to lever.

Top right: Fig. 16.15. Filling oil into the reservoir for bleeding.

Bottom right: Fig. 16.16. Opening and closing bleed connection at caliper.

Below: Fig. 16.14. Hydraulic oil reservoir opened up for bleeding the system.

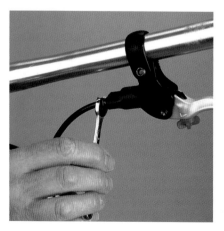

17

HUB BRAKE MAINTENANCE

Brakes that are integrated with the hub of the wheel, instead of working on the rim or on a disk, are referred to as hub brakes.

HUB BRAKE TYPES

The old standby for the American cruisers, and still very common in places like Holland and Germany, is the coaster brake. However, there are also other, more sophisticated brakes that fall in the category of hub brakes.

Both Shimano and SRAM offer such brakes for use on city bikes. Shimano's version is referred to as a roller brake, while SRAM's version is known as an internally expanding drum brake.

In addition, there are separate screwed-on drum brakes (requiring the use of a matching special hub with screw-thread) for tandem use as a third brake. Then there is the band brake, common on Japanese commuter bikes.

Left: Fig. 17.1. Drum brake.

Top right: Fig. 17.2. Roller brake.

Bottom right: Fig. 17.3. Coaster brake.

In this chapter, you will be shown how to deal with the typical maintenance and repair work that may be required on the various kinds of hub brakes. If the mechanism itself fails, it will be best to take it to a bike shop and have them deal with it. (Usually the advice will be to replace the brake rather than try to fix it.)

PRINCIPLE OF OPERATION

What all hub brakes have in common is that the wheel's rotation is retarded by a friction mechanism inside the wheel hub. There are two basic categories: those that are operated by means of levers and those that are operated by pedaling back. The latter are called coaster brakes in the U.S., backpedaling brakes in Britain.

There are several distinct types of lever-operated hub brakes: drum brakes, roller brakes, and band brakes.

The part that is fixed and to which the brake element is attached has to be firmly anchored by means of a counter-lever at some place on the frame some distance away. This counter-lever

also serves as the mounting point for the termination of the outer cable (except in the case of the coaster brake, of course).

In the case of the drum brake and the coaster brake, there is a set of high-friction segments inside the hub (or inside an enlarged part of the hub) that are pushed apart against the inside of the hub when the brake is applied. In the case of the roller brake, there is a set of rollers that rise up on ramps to press against the inside of the hub.

The band brake, finally, relies on a strap that engages the outside of a drum on the hub, and is usually controlled by means of a brake lever via a cable.

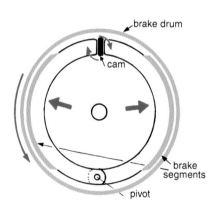
Fig. 17.5. Drum brake operation.

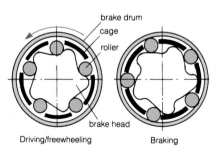
Fig. 17.6. Roller brake operation.

BRAKE TEST

To check operation of any of these brakes, you can follow the procedure *Brake Test* in Chapter 15, where it was described for rim brakes. However, be prepared to encounter the following differences:

1. Roller brakes and coaster brakes are not very suitable for gradual braking. Therefore be prepared to encounter a more sudden reaction, with the brake grabbing rather vigorously at an early point in their application.

2. All these brake types are much more subject to overheating on long descents than rim brakes are, with the result that you can't really predict how well these brakes work when you are riding fast in hilly terrain. In fact, I'd say that, though hub brakes are

Above: Fig. 17.7. Drum brake dismantled.

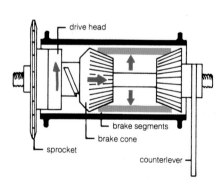
Fig. 17.4. Coaster brake operation.

perfectly suitable for most urban cycling, they should not be used for long-distance touring.

BRAKE ADJUSTMENT

Except for the coaster brake, all hub brakes can be adjusted by means of an adjuster quite similar to the ones found on the various types of rim brakes. Consequently, you are referred to the relevant steps in the description *Brake Adjustments* in Chapter 15.

BRAKE CABLE & LEVER MAINTENANCE

This operation is quite similar to what was described in Chapter 15 for rim brakes, both for the cable and the lever. Refer to the relevant procedures in that chapter.

COUNTER-LEVER PROBLEMS

This lever, which is common to all hub brakes, must be firmly attached to the left-side chainstay or fork blade (for rear and front brake respectively). Check its mounting bolt(s) from time to time, and tighten if necessary.

This is also a part that will have to be loosened in order to remove the wheel—and tight-

ened again properly upon reinstallation of the wheel. If it is not bolted directly to a welded-on plate on the frame or the fork, it is attached to a clamp that's wrapped around the left-side chainstay or fork blade. Make sure this clamp fits properly—if it can't be tightened properly, wrap something around the tube where the clamp goes, so that all slack is taken up. You can usually get a neoprene strip for this purpose, but if not, you can use a strip cut from an old inner tube.

There is one problem that may occur if the frame or, more typically, the front fork is not designed with a hub brake in mind. The force at the mounting point for the counter-lever can be quite high, and if the fork or the frame is not designed for it, it may bend or buckle at this location.

This is most typically the case if the lever is held with a clamp instead of being attached to a welded-on plate (because, if a manufacturer takes the trouble of welding on a plate, he'll know it's for a hub brake, and probably makes it strong enough for that

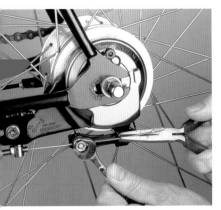

Above: Fig. 17.10. Adjusting drum brake.

Top left: Fig. 17.8. Adjusting roller brake cable.

Bottom left: Fig. 17.9. Clamping in cable at a different point to extend adjusting range.

Bottom right: Fig. 17.11. Unhooking cable anchor in cable stop for wheel removal.

kind of use). Check to make sure your hub brake is not bending the fork or the chainstays—and replace the drum brakes by regular rim brakes if the frame seems to be too light to take this kind of abuse. In fact, if there is obvious damage, you should replace the

entire fork or frame, because it'll not be safe.

HUB BRAKE BIKE GEAR ADAPTATIONS

Yes, even on a one-speed bike with a coaster brake or other type

of hub brake, it's possible to achieve a lower or a higher gear ratio. Of course, you'll be stuck with that higher or lower gear ratio all the time. If you find the bike is geared too high or too low, you can replace the freewheel cog by one of a different size. To get a lower gear, replace the cog by a bigger one. For a higher gear, choose a smaller cog. Fig. 17.15 shows how to do it. For detailed instructions, refer to Chapter 10, where this is described in some detail for the replacement of the cog on a hub gear unit.

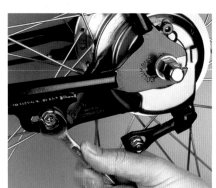

Above: Fig. 17.14. Simple coaster brake counter levers are attached with a clip around the chainstay.

Top left: Fig. 17.12. Installing roller brake counter lever to a stop on the chainstay.

Bottom left: Fig. 17.13. Tightening counter-lever bolt.

Right: Fig. 17.15. Replacing sprocket to achieve a different gear.

18

HANDLEBAR & STEM MAINTENANCE

There are two distinct handlebar types: "drop" handlebars, for use on road bikes, and flat bars, for use on mountain bikes and most other bicycle types.

HANDLEBAR & STEM DETAILS

The handlebars themselves are usually connected to the bike's steering system, consisting of front fork and headset bearings, via a stem that is clamped to the front fork's steerer tube and around the center portion of the handlebars.

After the brake levers are installed on the bars, the drop bars get wrapped with handlebar tape, while flat bars get equipped with handgrips pushed over the ends.

The handlebars are held in the stem by means of a clamp integrated in the stem that is held by means of one or two Allen bolts. How the stem attaches to the fork's steerer tube depends on the type of headset used on the bike in question (see Chapter 19).

On bikes with a conventional threaded headset, the stem is held in the fork's steerer tube by means of a wedge (or sometimes a conical item) that in turn is clamped in with a binder bolt reached from the top of the stem. On bikes with a threadless headset, the stem is clamped around an extension of the fork's steerer tube that sticks out above the upper headset.

Above: Fig. 18.2. Handlebar and stem on a bike with threadless headset.

Left: Fig. 18.1. Handlebar and stem on a bike with threaded headset.

ADJUST HANDLEBAR HEIGHT

This simplest of all handlebar adaptations only works on bikes with a conventional threaded headset. On bikes with a threadless headset, the only way to raise or lower the handlebars is by means of installing a different stem.

TOOLS & EQUIPMENT:

- Allen wrench (or, for older low-end bikes, regular wrench)

- mallet (or a hammer and a protective block of wood)

PROCEDURE:

1. Clamp the front wheel between your legs from the front and loosen the binder bolt on top of the stem by about 5 turns.

2. Tap on the bolt with a mallet (or a hammer, protecting the bolt with a block of wood) to loosen the wedge inside the stem—the bolt will drop down, loosening the stem.

3. Raise or lower the handlebars as desired and hold them there firmly.

4. Check to make sure the marking that shows the maximum extension of the stem does not show above the headset. If it does, lower the stem until it doesn't, because raising it too high might cause it to break or come loose.

5. Holding the handlebars at the desired height and straight (still clamping the front wheel between your legs), tighten the bolt on top of the stem firmly.

NOTE:

At least 2½ inches (6.5 cm) of the stem must remain clamped in.

Usually, the stem is marked for this insertion depth, but even if it's not, that's the minimum for safety.

ADJUST HANDLEBAR ANGLE

Especially for drop handlebars, this adjustment allows you to find a more comfortable rotation of the handlebars, if needed.

TOOLS & EQUIPMENT:

- Allen wrench (or for older models, regular wrench)

PROCEDURE:

1. Undo the clamp bolt(s) that hold the stem clamp around the handlebars by about one turn.

2. Turn the handlebars into the desired orientation, making sure they remain centered on the stem.

3. Holding the bars in the desired orientation and location, tighten the stem clamp bolt(s).

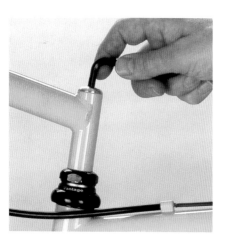

Above: Fig. 18.4. Loosening or tightening handlebar clamp bolt, e.g. to adjust handlebar angle.

Left: Fig. 18.3. Loosening or tightening handlebar stem on a bike with threaded headset, e.g. to adjust handlebar height.

Right: Fig. 18.5. Loosening or tightening handlebar clamp bolt on a bike with threadless headset.

REPLACE HANDLEBARS

Do this work if the handlebars are damaged in a fall or when you want to install a different type. Before proceeding, make sure the new handlebars actually fit the stem that's installed on the bike (or replace the stem as well.

TOOLS & EQUIPMENT:

- Allen wrench (or, for older low-end bikes, regular wrench)

- whatever tools are needed to remove items installed on the handlebars.

- sometimes large screw driver

PROCEDURE:

1. Remove anything installed on the handlebars (such as brake levers, gear shifters, handgrips or handlebar tape, etc.).

2. Unscrew the bolt(s) that hold the clamp on the stem around

the center section of the handlebars.

3. Pull the handlebars out, wiggling and rotating them until they come out. (You may have to pry open the clamp with the aid of a large screwdriver to get enough clearance.)

4. Tighten the clamp bolt(s) when the handlebars are in the right location and orientation.

5. Reinstall all items that were removed in Step 1.

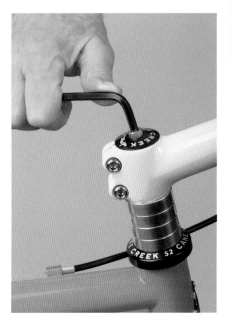

Above: Fig. 18.7. Above, Loosening or tightening the bolts that clamp the stem around the fork's steerer tube on a bike with threadless headset.

Left: Fig. 18.6. Removing or installing bolt on top of stem used with threadless headset. This bolt is used to adjust the headset bearings and should not get tightened, but it must be removed to remove the stem.

Right: Fig. 18.8. Stem removed from a bike with threaded headset.

REPLACE STEM

This operation may be needed if the stem that's on the bike brings the handlebars too far forward or not far enough, or—especially in combination with a threadless headset—too low or too high. If it's too long, you want one with less "reach"; if it's too low, one with more "rise." Make sure you get a replacement stem of the same general type (i.e. for the same type and size of steerer tube and the same diameter handlebars).

You'll also have to remove the handlebars from the stem and reinstall them when you've finished.

TOOLS & EQUIPMENT:

- Allen wrenches (or, for older low-end bikes, regular wrench)

- mallet (or a hammer and a protective block of wood)

- for threaded headset: cloth and lubricant

PROCEDURE:

1. Establish whether this is a bike with a threaded or threadless

headset (compare the illustrations).

• On a threaded headset, undo the bolt on top of the stem by about 5 turns and then tap on the bolt with a mallet (or a hammer and a protective block of wood) to loosen the stem.

• On a threadless headset, first undo the Allen bolt on the top of the stem (which is only an adjusting bolt), then remove this bolt and the underlying plastic cap, and finally loosen the bolts that clamp the stem around the fork's steerer tube extension that sticks out above the upper headset bearing.

2. Remove the old stem.

3. Open the bolts on the new stem (if it's for a threaded headset: far enough so the wedge or cone is loose enough to line up perfectly with the stem).

• On a threaded headset, put some lubricant on the screw-threaded portion of the

bolt and the wedge or cone, then place the new stem in place and orient it properly.

• On a threadless headset, put the stem in place, after installing any spacers required; but don't tighten the bolts that clamp it around the fork's smooth steerer tube extension yet. Install the cap and the bolt on top, and use the bolt to adjust the headset (refer to Chapter 19 for instructions), and only then tighten those clamp bolts.

4. While firmly holding the handlebars in place, tighten the bolt(s).

5. After you've installed the handlebars, make any final adjustments necessary and tighten all bolts.

SUSPENSION STEMS

This is the simplest, and surprisingly effective way of adding front suspension. You can replace a normal rigid stem by one of these, following the procedure outlined above for a regular stem.

The cheapest variety has an elastomer bumper to absorb the road shocks, whereas more sophisticated models have a pivoted parallelogram and a coil spring as well as some form of damping. You can adjust the spring rate and damping by tightening or loosening an Allen bolt.

By way of maintenance, they need to be kept clean, and any pivot points lubricated. The models with an elastomer bumper should not be left outside too long, because the elastomer would quickly deteriorate if exposed to sunlight too long.

REPLACE HANDGRIPS

Handgrips are used on flat handlebars, as used on mountain bikes and city bikes. Replace them if the old grips are not comfortable—or if you have to replace the brake lever, the gear shifter, the handlebars, or the stem.

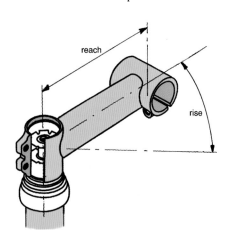

Fig. 18.9. Stem dimensions.

Above: Fig. 18.10. Adjusting the preload on a suspension stem.

Right: Fig. 18.11. Removing a handgrip from a flat-handlebar bike.

TOOLS & EQUIPMENT:

- screwdriver

- sometimes hot water, dishwashing liquid, hair spray, and a knife

PROCEDURE:

1. Remove the old handgrips by pulling and twisting—if they do not come off easily, place the screwdriver under the old grip and let some dishwashing liquid enter between the grip and the handlebars. If all else fails, cut the grip lengthwise and "peel" it off.

2. Push the new handgrips over the ends of the handlebars. If they don't go on easily, soak them in warm water first. To make them adhere better, you can spray some hair spray inside the grips just before installing them.

INSTALL BAR-ENDS

bar-ends are forward pointing extensions that can be installed at the ends of flat mountain bike handle-

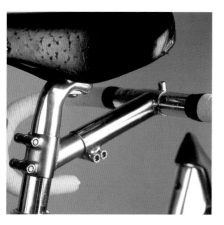

bars to offer the rider an alternative riding position. They're clamped around the ends of the handlebars. Since these things may form a potential hazard in a fall if they stick straight out, look for a model that curves in and has flexible protection at the ends.

TOOLS & EQUIPMENT:

- Allen wrench

PROCEDURE:

1. Remove the existing handgrips, and replace them with open-ended grips, pushed about ¾ inch (2 cm) further to the center of the bars. (Alternately, you can cut the ends off the existing ones and slide them in that far).

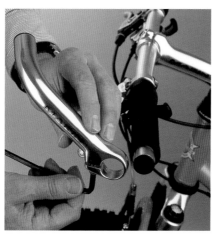

Above: Fig. 18.13. Installing bar ends on a mountain bike handlebar.

Left: Fig. 18.12. Special tandem "stoker" stem, attached to the front seatpost. This one is adjustable in length.

Top right: Fig. 18.14. Locating the brake lever before taping the handlebars.

Bottom right: Fig. 18.15. Wrapping around the brake mount.

2. Place the bar-ends over the uncovered ends of the handlebars, with the clamping bolts underneath—the extensions pointing forward and slightly up (by about 15–30 degrees).

3. Adjust them so that both point up under the same angle, then tighten the clamp bolts very firmly.

4. Ride the bike and do any fine-tuning that may be necessary.

REPLACE HANDLEBAR TAPE

Replace the tape used on road bike handlebars when it becomes tat-

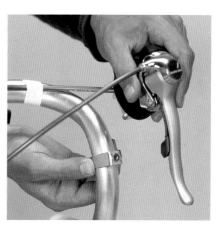

tered or uncomfortable—and when you need to replace either the bars themselves, the stem, or one of the items installed on the handlebars. If available, choose a type of tape that is thicker in the middle than at the sides. If it has adhesive backing, it should only be in the middle portion.

TOOLS & EQUIPMENT:

- screwdriver (for some bar-end plugs)
- knife or scissors

PROCEDURE:

1. If the plugs have screws in the end, loosen the screws about 5 turns and remove the plugs by pulling and twisting.

    - If there are no screws, just pry them off.

2. Cut the tape at the end closest to the center of the bars and unwind the tape from the bars. At the brake levers, lift the rub-ber hoods far enough to get access to all the tape.

3. Make sure the brake levers are symmetrically mounted where they are comfortable to reach when riding.

4. If necessary, tape down the brake cable (and sometimes, e.g. on touring bikes with han-dlebar-end shifters, the derail-leur cable) at 4-inch (10 cm) intervals.

5. Place a 4-inch (10 cm) section of tape across the brake lever mounting strap.

6. Starting at the ends, where you tuck in the first inch of tape, wrap the bars inward, overlap-ping each subsequent layer half-way with the next layer.

7. Cross-wrap at the brake levers and continue straight to a point about 3 inches (about 7.5 cm) from the center.

8. Reinstall the bar-end plugs.

9. Wrap a 4-inch (10 cm) long piece of adhesive tape around the ends of the taped sections.

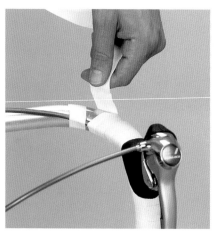

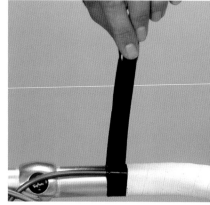

Above: Fig. 18.17. Taping last section of handlebars, covering brake cable.

Left: Fig. 18.16. Taping around the brake mounts.

Top right: Fig. 18.18. Covering the end of the taping with adhesive tape.

Bottom right: Fig. 18.19. Installing the handlebar end plugs.

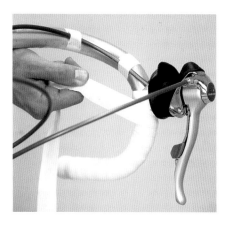

19
HEADSET MAINTENANCE

The headset is what supports the bike's steering system. It consists of an upper and a lower set of ball bearings, mounted in the top and the bottom of the frame's head tube respectively.

HEADSET TYPES

Unlike other bearings on the bike, the headset bearings get most of their wear from road shocks par-allel to their axis, referred to as axial loading. Therefore at least the lower bearing must be a so-called axial bearing (as opposed to the regular radial bearings used elsewhere on the bike).

Two different headset types are in common use: threaded and threadless. The conventional threaded bearing has an adjustable bearing race that is screwed onto the fork's steerer tube. The currently more common threadless headset is adjusted from the top of the handlebar stem. There is also something called an integrated headset, which is basically

Above: Fig. 19.2. Threadless headset.

Left: Fig. 19.1. Steering system overview.

Right: Fig. 19.3. Threaded headset.

(Labels in Fig. 19.1: handlebars, hand grip, upper headset, stem, head tube, bottom headset, front fork)

a threadless headset made up of fewer parts, with the bearings installed directly in the frame's head tube. Comparing the illustrations will help you define which type is installed on the bike you're working on.

Maintenance work on the headset includes adjusting, overhauling, and replacing the bearings. These operations are different for the two major types of headsets. Some of this work also has to be carried out when you have to replace e.g. the front fork.

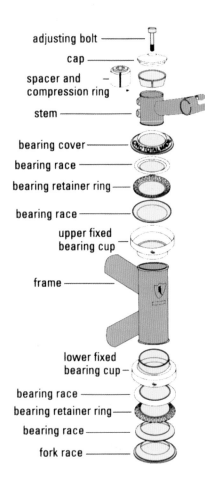

Fig. 19.4. Parts of the threadless headset.

THREADLESS HEADSETS

Threadless headsets are also referred to as AHeadset, which is Dia Compe's (the patent holder) model designation for this type of headset. Fig. 19.4 shows how it is built up and installed. It requires a fork that does not have screw thread on the steerer tube. The bolt on top of the stem does not hold the parts together but is merely there to adjust of the bearings.

Any instructions below for the threadless headset also apply to the integrated headset, which is nothing more than a variation on the same theme as the threadless headset.

ADJUST THREADLESS HEADSET

The threadless headset tends to stay properly adjusted longer, but there may still be a need for adjustment from time to time.

Above: Fig. 19.5. Loosening top bolt.

Right: Fig. 19.6. Loosening clamp bolts.

TOOLS & EQUIPMENT:

• Allen wrenches

PROCEDURE:

1. Loosen the clamp bolts that hold the stem around the fork's steerer tube by about one turn each.

2. Tighten or loosen the Allen bolt on top of the stem—this is not a binder bolt taking force but solely serves as an adjustment bolt (and the plastic or aluminum cap underneath would break if too much force were applied to it by that bolt). Tighten by turning the bolt clockwise, loosen by turning it counterclockwise.

3. When the adjustment feels right, tighten the stem clamp bolts, making sure the handlebars are straight.

OVERHAUL OR REPLACE THREADLESS HEADSET

These headsets rarely need maintenance work, but if they do give you trouble, you can take them apart and/or replace them. Before you start, remove the front wheel and unhook the front brake cable.

TOOLS & EQUIPMENT:

- Allen wrenches
- cloth
- bearing grease

DISASSEMBLY PROCEDURE:

1. Undo the Allen bolt on top of the stem and remove it, together with the underlying cap.

2. Holding the fork and the bottom of the head tube together, loosen the bolts that clamp the stem around the top portion of the fork's steerer tube; then remove the stem.

3. Pull the fork out of the head tube, catching the bearing balls.

OVERHAULING PROCEDURE:

1. Clean and inspect all parts, and replace any parts that are damaged, corroded, pitted, or grooved. If you have to replace individual parts or the entire headset, it's best to take the fork with you to the shop to make sure you get parts of the correct size to match the fork's steerer tube diameter.

2. If you have to replace the entire headset, it will be best to have a bike shop install the fixed components (the fixed upper and lower bearing races and the fork race), because that job is best done with special tools that any bike shop should have but for which you don't have a use often

Left: Fig. 19.7. Bolt and cap removed.

Above: Fig. 19.8. The "star-fangled" washer.

Right: Fig. 19.9. The stem removed.

enough to justify the investment.

INSTALLATION PROCEDURE:

1. Fill the upper and lower fixed bearing races with bearing grease.

2. Holding the frame upside down, put the retainer ring with the bearing balls in the lower fixed race, which is now on top.

3. Holding the fork upside down as well, insert the fork's steerer tube through the frame's head tube until the bearing balls of the lower headset bearing are securely held between the fork race and the lower fixed race.

4. Turn the bike the right way round, carefully holding the fork and the lower part of the head tube together.

5. Still holding things together with one hand, first put the retainer ring with the bearing balls into the upper fixed

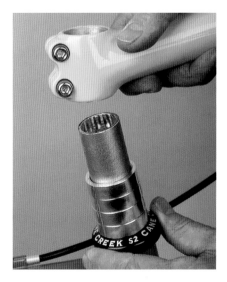

bearing race and then slide the adjustable bearing race onto the fork's steerer tube.

6. Install the slotted, tapered ring (or two tapered segments) in the gap and place the washer on top. Install any other spacers that may be used to raise the handlebars, then slide the stem on and provisionally screw the stem clamp bolts just enough to hold things together but free to slide.

7. Install the cap on top of the stem and attach it loosely with the Allen bolt on top, screwing the latter into what the manufacturer refers to as a "star-fangled washer" (which is really a nut, because it has internal screw thread) inside the fork's steerer tube.

8. Adjust the bearing with the Allen bolt on top of the stem (clockwise to tighten, counter-clockwise to loosen the bearing), then tighten the stem clamp bolts with the handlebars in the correct orientation.

NOTE:

If the "star-fangled" washer" is pushed too far into the steerer tube, or if it goes under an angle, you can push it out from the bottom (holding the fork upside-down) with a large screwdriver and a hammer or a mallet. Then have a bike shop push it (or a replacement) in again from the top, which requires a special tool.

INTEGRATED HEADSET NOTE:

Integrated headsets work just like the threadless headset. The only difference is that the bearing races are permanently integrated with the head tube and the parts just slide into place. For adjustment, removal, overhaul, and installation, you can follow the same procedure, as for the threaded headset.

Above: Fig. 19.11. Installing spacers to raise the handlebar.

Left: Fig. 19.10. The fork pulled out of the head tube, exposing the lower bearing race seat.

THREADED HEADSETS

Fig. 19.12 shows the way a threaded headset is built up and installed. It requires a fork with a threaded steerer tube.

ADJUST THREADED HEADSET

If the bearings are too tight or too loose, first try to adjust them. If that does not solve the problem, you'll have to proceed to the instructions for overhauling, or even replacing, the headset.

TOOLS & EQUIPMENT:

- headset wrenches (make sure they're the size to match the make and model in question)

- sometimes a large adjustable wrench can be used as a substitute for a specific size headset wrench

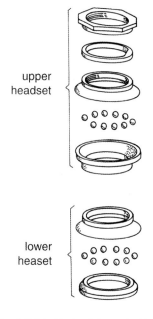

upper headset

lower heaset

Fig. 19.12. Parts of threaded headset.

- sometimes a tiny Allen wrench, if there's a grub screw to hold down the bearing locknut

PROCEDURE:

1. Loosen the locknut on top of the upper headset bearing about one turn (unless there is a toothed ring underneath, on some older headsets—in that case far enough to free those teeth). If the locknut is held with a grub screw, loosen that little screw before trying to undo the locknut.

2. Lift the keyed washer that lies under the locknut to allow the adjustable bearing race to be rotated.

3. Turn the adjustable bearing race in $1/8$-turn increments (clockwise to tighten, counterclockwise to loosen) until it feels just barely loose (that slack will get taken up when the locknut is screwed down).

4. Tighten the locknut fully while holding the adjustable race with the other wrench.

5. Check to make sure the bearing is properly adjusted now, or fine-tune the adjustment if necessary, then tighten the locknut firmly.

OVERHAUL OR REPLACE THREADED HEADSET

Do this work when the steering has become rough and the problem cannot be solved by simply adjusting the headset bearings in accordance with the preceding instructions. Before starting, remove the handlebar stem from the bike, following the procedure in Chapter 18. Also remove the front wheel and unhook the front brake cable.

TOOLS & EQUIPMENT:

- headset wrenches or substitute wrenches

- sometimes a tiny Allen wrench if there's a grub screw to hold down the bearing locknut

- cloth

- bearing grease

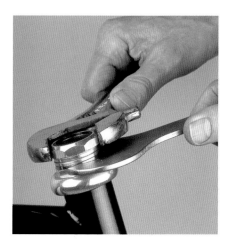

Above: Fig. 19.13. Adjusting or disassembling the threaded headset bearings.

Right: Fig. 19.14. Retainer with bearing balls in the upper headset bearing.

DISASSEMBLY PROCEDURE:

1. Loosen and remove the locknut on top of the upper headset (if appropriate, after unscrewing a grub screw that may be present on some models).

2. Lift and remove the keyed washer from the fork's screw-threaded steerer tube. The steerer tube has a matching groove or flat spot cut into the screw thread, which prevents rotation of the washer.

3. Hold the fork and the frame together at the fork crown. Then unscrew the adjustable bearing race (after loosening a grub screw, if installed).

4. Remove the bearing balls from the upper fixed bearing race (usually held in a retainer).

5. Pull the fork out of the frame, catching the bearing balls (usually also in a retainer) from the lower headset bearing.

OVERHAULING PROCEDURE:

1. Clean and inspect all parts, replacing any parts that are damaged, corroded, pitted, or grooved. A particular problem to watch for is "brinelling" of a bearing surface, i.e. pitting caused by repeated impact at the same point (most prevalent at the lower headset bearing).

   • When replacing parts (or, for that matter, when replacing an entire headset) be aware that they come in different sizes—take the fork with you to the shop to get one that's guaranteed to fit.

2. If the entire headset has to be replaced, it will be best to have a bike shop remove and install the fixed components (the upper and lower cups on the head tube and the fork race on the fork crown), because those jobs are best done with special tools.

INSTALLATION PROCEDURE:

1. Fill the upper and lower fixed bearing races with bearing grease.

2. Holding the frame upside down, put the bearing balls (usually in a retainer) in the lower fixed bearing race (which is now on top).

3. Holding the fork upside down as well, push the fork's steerer tube through until the bearing balls of the lower headset bearing are securely held between the fork race and the lower fixed race.

4. Turn the bike the right way round, carefully holding the fork crown and the lower part of the head tube together.

5. Still holding things together with one hand, put the bearing balls (also usually in a retainer) into the upper fixed bearing race, then screw the adjustable bearing race onto the fork's steerer tube until the bearing is just a tad loose.

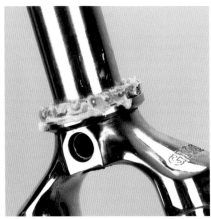

Above: Fig. 19.16. Lower bearing with lubricated bearing retainer.

Left: Fig. 19.15. Lubricating bearing.

Right: Fig. 19.17. Headset bearing with a grub screw.

6. Install the keyed washer on the adjustable bearing race, matching the prong or the flat part of the washer up with the groove or flat area on the threaded portion of the steerer tube. Also install any other items that may have to go between the lock washer and the locknut (e.g. spacer, cantilever brake stop, or reflector mounting bracket).

7. Holding the adjustable bearing cup with one tool, install and tighten the locknut fully.

8. Check whether the headset is now adjusted properly (i.e. free to rotate without resistance on the one hand or looseness—or "play"— on the other, and adjust if necessary.

CARTRIDGE BEARING NOTE:

Some conventional-looking headsets on high-end bikes are equipped with cartridge bearings. They can't be adjusted, and you'll have to get them replaced at a bike shop if they do give you trouble (but don't worry, they can handle many years of hard use).

SADDLE & SEATPOST MAINTENANCE

The saddle, or seat, is usually made of a firm but flexible plastic base, held on a metal frame, with a real or simulated leather cover over a thin layer of padding.

SADDLE TYPES

Racing saddles are narrow and firm, while saddles intended for an upright riding position tend to be wide and soft (or rather: not quite so rock hard). Some sad-dles are made of self-supporting thick and firm leather, directly connected to the metal frame.

The saddle is held on the bike by means of a tubular seatpost, which is clamped in at the seat lug, at the top of the frame's seat tube. Different inside diameters of seat tubes call for seatposts with (slightly) different outside diameters. The seat lug and the top of the seat tube are split in the back and tightened around the seatpost with a clamp, which is either bolted to-gether or clamped with a quick-release device.

ADJUST SEAT HEIGHT

Once you've determined how high you want the saddle to be, this is how you get it there.

TOOLS & EQUIPMENT:

- Depending on the type of clamp, either none (if quick-release), an Allen wrench (modern quality bike),

Left: Fig. 20.1. Saddle and seatpost on a mountain bike with quick-release seatpost binder bolt.

Right: Fig. 20.2. Adjusting the seat height on a road bike with regular binder bolt.

or a regular wrench (older or low-end bike)

PROCEDURE:

1. Depending on the type of saddle clamp:

   • On a bike with a regular bolted clamp, undo the bolt (referred to as binder bolt) by 2–3 turns.

   • On a bike with quick-release clamp, twist the quick-release lever into the "open" position.

2. Try to move the seatpost up or down in a twisting movement, using the saddle for leverage while holding the bike's frame. If it doesn't budge, squirt some penetrating oil in at the point where the seat lug is slotted, so it enters between the seatpost and the seat tube. Wait 2–3 minutes and try again.

3. Move it to the exact location where you want it to be, but make sure the marker that shows the minimum insertion depth is not exposed (if it is, it'll be dangerous to ride that way, and you'll need either a longer seatpost or a bigger frame).

4. Holding the saddle at the right height and straight ahead, tighten the binder bolt or the quick-release. (If the quick-release can't be tightened properly, flip it to "open" again, adjust the thumb nut on the other side, and try again.)

5. Check to make sure the position is correct, and fine-tune the various adjustments if necessary.

   • You may find that you now need to adjust the angle and

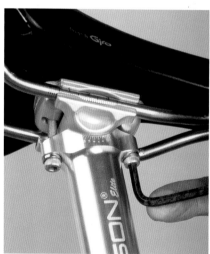

forward position in accordance with the instructions below as well.

NOTE:

At least 2½ inches (6.5 cm) of the seatpost must be clamped in. Usually the seatpost is marked to show this minimum safe insertion depth.

ADJUST SEAT ANGLE & FORWARD POSITION

These features are adjusted by means of one or more bolts, usually accessible from underneath the saddle, that hold the saddle wires to the seatpost.

TOOLS & EQUIPMENT:

• Allen wrench (or sometimes a regular wrench for an older bike)

Procedure:

1. Look under the saddle and identify the bolts in question; usually they're easily accessi-

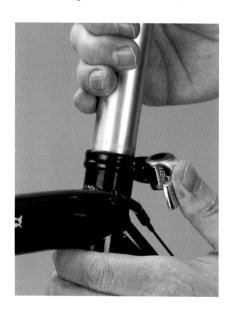

Above: Fig. 20.4. Adjusting saddle angle and/or forward position.

Left: Fig. 20.3. Operating quick-release binder bolt.

Right: Fig. 20.5. Installing seat on seatpost.

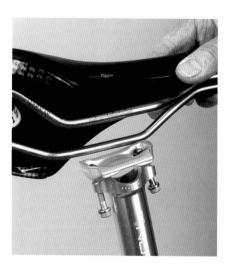

ble from below, but on older models, they can be tricky to reach (between the saddle cover and the clamp). On low-end bikes there's one nut on either side of the wires (or the flat rails often used on such saddles).

2. Loosen the bolts about 3 turns.

3. Move the saddle forward or backward on the wires, while making sure the clamp does not run off those wires, and hold it at the desired location under the desired angle.

4. Holding the saddle steadily in place, tighten the bolts, gradually tightening both of them in turn if there are two.

5. Check to make sure the position is correct, and fine-tune the various adjustments if necessary (it may also have affected the height adjustment).

REPLACE SADDLE

To do this work, e.g. because you want to try a more comfortable model, you can either leave the seatpost clamped in at the bike or you can work on it while it's off the bike.

TOOLS & EQUIPMENT:

• Allen wrench (or sometimes a regular wrench on an older bike)

PROCEDURE:

1. Look under the saddle and identify the bolts in question; usually they're easily accessible from below, but they can be tricky to get at on older models.

2. Loosen the bolts far enough to twist the saddle off the clip.

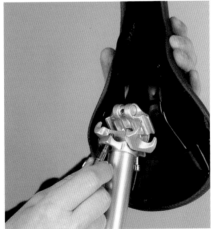

Above: Fig. 20.7. Removing the saddle from the seatpost clip.

Left: Fig. 20.6. Grease the seatpost before inserting it in the seat tube.

Right: Fig. 20.8. Assembling the seatpost clip.

3. Install the new saddle on the clamp and hold it loosely with the bolts or nuts.

4. Move the saddle forward or backward on the wires (while making sure the clamp does not run off those wires) and hold it in the desired location under the desired angle.

5. Holding the saddle steadily in place, tighten the bolts, gradually tightening them in turn.

6. Check to make sure the position is correct, and fine-tune the various adjustments if necessary.

REPLACE SEATPOST

To remove the seatpost, leave the saddle on the seatpost and remove the two together as a single unit, then take the seatpost off the saddle.

TOOLS & EQUIPMENT:

• Depending on the type of clamp, either none (if

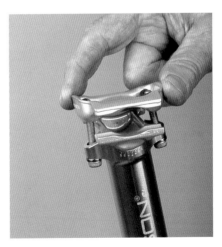

quick-release), an Allen wrench, or a regular wrench (older or low-end bike)

- cloth
- grease
- sometimes penetrating oil

PROCEDURE:

1. Depending on the type of clamp:

   • On a bike with a bolted clamp, undo the binder bolt 2–3 turns.

   • On a bike with a quick-release clamp, twist the quick-release lever into the "open" position.

2. Try to move the seatpost up in a twisting movement, using the saddle for leverage. If it doesn't budge, squirt some penetrating oil in at the point where the seat lug is slotted, so it enters between the seatpost and the seat tube. Wait 2–3 minutes and try again. Pull the seatpost all the way out.

INSTALLATION PROCEDURE:

Do this after the saddle has been installed on the new seatpost.

1. Apply grease to the inside of the seat tube and the outside of the seatpost.

2. Insert the seatpost in the seat tube.

3. Move it to the exact location where you want it to be, but make sure the marker that shows the minimum insertion depth is not exposed.

4. Holding the saddle at the right height and straight ahead, tighten the binder bolt or the quick-release. (If the quick-release can't be tightened properly, flip it to "open" again, adjust the thumb nut

on the other side, and try again.)

5. Check to make sure the position is correct, and fine-tune the various adjustments if necessary. You may find that you now need to readjust the angle and forward position.

NOTE:

At least 2½ inches (6.5 cm) of the seatpost must be clamped in. Usually the seatpost is marked to show this safe insertion depth.

SUSPENSION SEATPOSTS

These items are surprisingly effective in helping to smooth the ride on "hardtail" bikes, i.e. those without "real" rear suspension. However, a word of warning is in order here: never use a suspension seatpost on a bike *with* rear suspension, because the effect of the two suspension methods against each other may ruin the more sophisticated rear suspension element. For relevant suspension terminology, see Chapter 22.

Left: Fig. 20.9. Externally adjustable suspension seatpost.

Above: Fig. 20.10. Rebound adjustment from underneath, but make sure some thread remains exposed.

Right: Fig. 20.11. Parts of suspension seatpost.

Preload is the only factor that can be adjusted on the suspension seatpost. To do that, remove the seatpost from the bike, and use an Allen wrench to tighten or loosen the adjuster plug in the bottom of the seatpost. Turning it in tightens the initial compression of the spring element inside; turning it out slackens it. Don't unscrew it so far that any part of the adjuster plug extends from the seatpost end (at least the beginning of the internal screw threads in the seatpost must be visible).

MAINTENANCE OF LEATHER SADDLE

A real leather saddle stretches with use, especially if it is allowed to get wet. The best way to maintain its integrity is to treat the cover with leather grease (available from the saddle manufacturer, but any mineral oil or grease will do in a pinch; just

don't use vegetable oil) once or twice a year. Let it sit overnight so it penetrates properly before using the seat. Occasionally, you may also have to tension the saddle cover to account for stretch.

TOOLS & EQUIPMENT:

- special saddle wrench available from the saddle manufacturer (i.e. probably Brooks, the major surviving leather saddle manufacturer)

PROCEDURE:

1. Look under the saddle cover near the tip (referred to as the "nose" of the saddle) and identify the bolt that holds the tip of the saddle cover to the

wires, then find the nut on this bolt for adjusting.

2. Tighten the nut by about ½ turn at a time until the saddle cover has the right tension. Do not overtighten.

REVIVING A SAGGING LEATHER SADDLE:

If the saddle cover "sags," flaring out at the sides near the front, you can usually rescue it as follows:

1. Drill a series of four or five $3/32$-inch (2 mm) diameter holes about ¾ inch (20 mm) apart, about ½ inch (12 mm) above the lower edge on both sides of the flared-out area.

2. Using a thin round shoe lace, tie the two sides together into an acceptable shape and tie the ends of the shoe lace together in a firm knot kept out of sight.

Above: Fig. 20.13. Installation of sprung leather saddle by means of an adaptor plate.

Left: Fig. 20.12. Adjusting the tension of a leather saddle cover.

Right: Fig. 20.14. "Lacing up" a sagging leather saddle cover.

21 FRAME & FORK MAINTENANCE

Although the frameset (i.e. the frame with the front fork) is the biggest of the bicycle's components, it's not really subject to the kind of damage that calls for repair and maintenance very much.

The few things that can happen—and the even fewer things that can be done about them—are covered in this chapter.

FRAME CONSTRUCTION

Most frames are made up of aluminum tubing, welded together into a roughly diamond-shaped structure. The frame itself comprises the main frame, built up from large diameter tubing, and the rear triangle made of smaller diameter tubing. The front fork is free to rotate in the main frame's head tube by means of the headset (see Chapter 19).

In recent years, frame construction and design have changed quite a bit, especially due to the use of different materi-als and the proliferation of suspension systems, especially on mountain bikes. As for materials, most frames are now made of aluminum alloys, while also titanium, carbon fiber, and magnesium are in use.

The problem with all those "new" materials is that frames and forks made with them are even less repairable than steel frames are. The kind of damage that a frame or a fork is likely to sustain is either so minor that it doesn't really matter much (e.g. scratched paint) or so major that it can't be fixed, and requires re-placement. Therefore this chapter mainly deals with checking for damage, rather than actually fixing things once they are dam-aged. The one thing you can

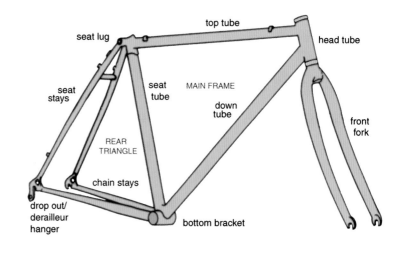

Fig. 21.1. The parts of the frame set.

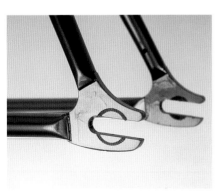

do—at least on a frame made of steel or welded aluminum—is touching up the paint, and that will be covered at the end of the chapter.

FRAME INSPECTION

The two most significant areas to watch out for are the front fork and the area of the downtube just behind the lower headset. If you see any bulging or cracking, check with the bike shop (whose advice is probably to discard the frame or the fork). If there is no obvious damage, check for distortion of frame and fork, as per the following procedures.

Above: Fig. 21.6. Reinforcement of the weakest point of a frame: where the downtube meets the head tube.

Left: Figs. 21.2 through 21.5. Dropout details, from top to bottom:

Fig. 21.2. Horizontal Campagnolo right-side dropout.

Fig. 21.3. Vertical Investment cast steel right-side dropout for high-end steel frame.

Fig. 21.4. Separate derailleur hanger for right-side dropout on aluminum frame.

Fig. 21.5. Track dropouts, as used on single-speed and "fixed-wheel" bikes.

FRAME ALIGNMENT CHECK

It's not safe to ride a bike with a frame that is misaligned, meaning that the front and rear wheels don't exactly follow one another in the same track. It negatively affects the balance of the bike, both when going straight and, even more unpredictably, when cornering. You can check the alignment of the frame yourself.

TOOLS & EQUIPMENT:

- 10 feet (3 m) of twine

- calipers (or straightedge with mm markings)

PROCEDURE:

1. Wrap the twine around the frame from the right-side rear dropout to the head tube, pull it around and run it back to the left-side dropout.

2. Measure the distance between the twine and the frame's seat tube on the right and the left and record the results.

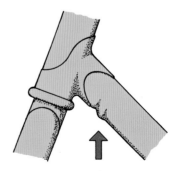

Fig. 21.7. Buckling damage at bottom of downtube-to-head-tube connection.

3. If the two measurements differ, the frame is misaligned—just how much is *too* much is up for debate, but I would say that any difference in excess of 3 mm (¹⁄₈ inch) is probably unsafe. At least take the bike to a bike shop and ask for advice.

DROPOUT ALIGNMENT CHECK

The dropouts (i.e. the flat plates on which the rear wheel is installed) should be parallel for the wheel to align properly.

TOOLS & EQUIPMENT:

- 18-inch (45 cm) metal straightedge

- calipers

PROCEDURE

1. Hold the metal straightedge perpendicular to one of the dropouts, extending in the direction of the seat tube and measure the distance between ruler and seat tube.

2. Do the same on the other dropout.

3. Compare the measurements. Again, there is some latitude for interpretation as to what constitutes unsafe misalignment, but I'd ask for professional advice at a bike shop if the difference is more than 3 mm (¹⁄₈ inch).

FORK INSPECTION

What matters here is the alignment of the two fork blades relative to each other and relative to the steerer tube. On a regular fork, you can usually check the alignment by means of a visual inspection.

TOOLS & EQUIPMENT:

- calipers

- flat, level surface

PROCEDURE:

1. Place the fork flat on the level surface, supporting it at the fork crown and the upper straight section of the fork blades.

2. Compare the distance between the level surface and the fork ends. If there's a difference, they're misaligned.

3. Visually establish whether the line that goes through the center of the steerer tube also goes through the center of the upper straight portion of the fork blades. If it doesn't, you have misalignment between the fork blades and the steerer tube.

4. Also in this case, once you have established that there is misalignment, go to a bike

Right and above: Figs. 21.8. and 21.9. Frame alignment inspection and measuring detail.

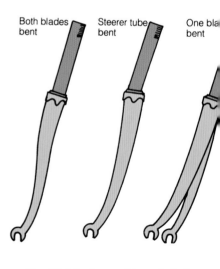

Fig. 21.10. Types of front fork damage

shop and get advice on what to do.

FRONT FORK INSTALLATION

To turn a loose frame and a separate fork into a frameset, you have to install the front fork in the frame. Most of the work involved is referenced in Chapter 19, which covers the headset, because the headset is the link between the frame and the fork.

First make sure that the headset fits both the fork's steerer tube and the frame's head tube. Not only is there the difference between threaded and threadless steerer tubes, depending on the type of headset used, there are also steerer tubes and headsets in different diameters.

Also the length of the steerer tube must add up to the height of the frame's head tube plus the "stacking height" of the headset (and the stem height plus any spacers in the case of a threadless headset).

Additionally, there's the distinction between regular forks and suspension forks. If you are trying to install a suspension fork in a frame not specifically designed for one, explain that at the

bike shop before buying the fork, because for safe handling, you should avoid altering the bike's steering geometry too much.

For all other details, see the installation procedure in Chapter 19 for the particular type of headset used.

PAINT TOUCH-UP

When a regular painted, brazed or welded metal frame or fork shows any scratches, you can touch up the paint to prevent rust and to keep the bike looking as nice as possible. Don't do this on carbon fiber frames, nor on a frame with bonded joints (as opposed to one that's brazed or welded), because the solvents used either in preparation or actual painting may weaken the epoxy, and possibly void the warranty.

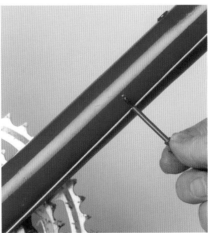

Above: Fig. 21.12. Frame paint touch-up.

Left: Fig. 21.11. Another kind of damage: bent brake pivot on a front fork—the same can happen on the frame itself.

TOOLS & EQUIPMENT:

- matching paint (if not available from the manufacturer, buy a close match in a model shop or an auto supply store)
- tiny brush
- steel wool or emery cloth
- paint thinner
- cloth

PROCEDURE:

1. Thoroughly clean the area of (and around) the damage.

2. Use emery cloth or a tiny speck of steel wool to remove corrosion, dirt, and paint remnants down to the bare, shiny metal surface.

3. Clean the area to be repainted once more with a cloth soaked in paint thinner, and wipe it dry.

4. Shake the paint thoroughly to mix it well.

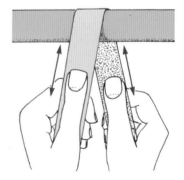

Fig. 21.13. Sanding frame tubes prior to painting.

5. Using the tiny brush, just barely dipped in paint, apply paint only to the damaged area.

6. Let it dry for at least 24 hours, and repeat Steps 4 and 5 if necessary.

REPAINTING FRAME & FORK

It's a major job, and hard to do just right. Don't try to do this on a composite bike, because it will void the warranty (and worse, it may damage the bonding materials used). On a conventional frame, it can be done, and here is how to go about it. Use automotive spray can paint.

Before you start, read the instructions on the can and follow them to the letter. But before you make a mess of the frame, practice on some old pieces of metal.

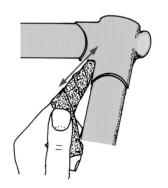

Fig. 21.14. Sanding in tight corners.

The trick is to pass the spray in a constant, overlapping pattern, starting before you reach the item to be painted, and finishing each pass beyond it.

PREPARATION PROCEDURE:

1. Remove everything from the bike (except perhaps the bottom bracket and the headset cups, providing you cover them well with masking tape).

2. Place plugs (e.g. corks or rolled-up paper) in the places where you don't want paint to enter, such as the seat lug, bottom bracket, and the head tube. Then clean the bike thoroughly.

3. Using either paint stripper or abrasive cloth, remove all traces of the old paint and rust. Then clean with paint thinner and allow to dry.

4. Hang the item to be painted as shown in Fig. 21.15 in a clean dust-free area with good ventilation.

PAINTING PROCEDURE:

1. Apply paint to the frame and/or the fork, working around systematically, covering all sides and angles

equally thoroughly. Use a spoke, hooked in a dropout eyelet to turn the frame or the fork.

FINISHING PROCEDURE:

1. Wait at least 24 hours, then check whether the paint is really "cured" (dry and hard) in an unobtrusive place.

2. Once the paint is cured, wait another 24 hours, and then use rubbing compound or paint polish to polish out the paint to an even shine.

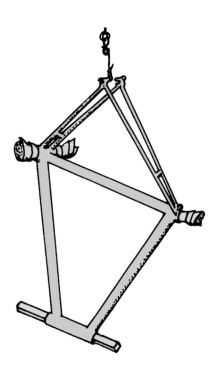

Fig. 21.15. Hanging up the painted frame to dry.

22
FRONT SUSPENSION MAINTENANCE

Since the early 1990s, there has been a trend toward the integration of suspension systems on bicycles. Nowadays, not only mountain bikes, where many modern systems were first used, but even city bicycles often come with some form of suspension.

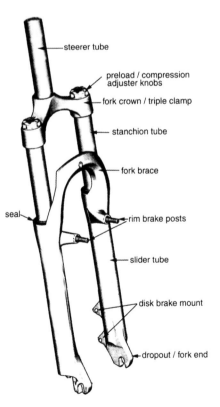

Fig. 22.1. Suspension fork terminology.

steerer tube

preload / compression adjuster knobs

fork crown / triple clamp

stanchion tube

fork brace

seal

rim brake posts

slider tube

disk brake mount

dropout / fork end

Sometimes this means no more than replacing a standard fork or seatpost by a sprung version of essentially the same item, without much change to the rest of the bike. However, in other cases, it means that the bicycle is designed specifically around a suspension system, giving it an entirely different look. In this chapter, we'll cover only front suspension, while the Chapter 23 is devoted to the rear suspension.

SUSPENSION TERMINOLOGY

What's commonly referred to as suspension really comprises two different but related concepts: suspension and damping. Think of the former as "springiness" and

the latter as a way of reducing "bounciness" after the suspension's first response to an impact.

If the fork responds immediately to the slightest bump and tends to spring right up again, it has inadequate damping. If it does not respond enough to an impact, it either has too much damping or the spring is too tough for the rider's weight. If it

Left: Fig. 22.2. Front suspension fork overview.

"bottoms out" even in response to moderate bumps, the spring element is too weak for the rider's weight.

The most important measure of suspension is called travel—the difference between the compressed and uncompressed state. You want more for downhill racing in rough terrain than for more modest use.

Two other concepts are preload and "stiction." Preload refers to the amount by which the spring element is compressed even before hitting a bump. Stiction is the initial resistance against movement. For rough terrain, you want more stiction than for a bike ridden mainly on relatively smooth paths. Preload should be no more than 25 percent of total travel.

SUSPENSION STEMS

This is the simplest, and surprisingly effective way of adding front

suspension. You can replace a normal rigid stem by one of these, following the procedure outlined in Chapter 18. Usually, preload is the only factor that can be adjusted on a suspension stem.

SUSPENSION FORKS

The most common front suspension is by means of a telescoping suspension fork. These incorporate two sets of tubes that slide inside each other, the inner ones (the stanchion tubes) being guided in the outer ones (called slider tubes) and connected with spring elements. The spring elements are either elastomer pads, metal coil springs, or air cartridges; and different types may be combined on different sides of the same fork. See Fig. 22.1 for the names of the parts of a suspension fork.

By way of preventive maintenance, the most important thing is to keep the seals and the stanchion tubes clean. Do this once a week and after every ride in wet weather or dusty terrain. Wipe the exposed parts of the stanchions and the seals; then apply synthetic oil to these parts and push the fork in five times; finally wipe the stanchion tubes clean once more.

In addition, check the suspension fork at least once a season to make sure it is working properly, as described under *Suspension Fork Check*.

SUSPENSION FORK CHECK

TOOLS & EQUIPMENT:

* Usually none required.

PROCEDURE:

1. Holding the bike firmly at the headset, try to wiggle the bottom of the fork at the fork-ends. If they move

Above: Fig. 22.4. Pressurizing valve on a fork with pneumatic suspension cartridges.

Left: Fig. 22.3. Cleaning and lubricating the stanchion tubes.

Right: Fig. 22.5. Typical suspension fork controls on top of the fork crown.

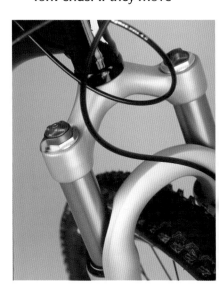

loosely, you have a problem, which you should refer to a bike shop mechanic.

2. Holding the bike from the front at the handlebars, push down with all your body weight and observe how the suspension fork reacts. If all is well, it goes down with increasing resistance but does not stop suddenly.

3. With the suspension fork pushed in as in step 2, release pressure and observe whether the recovery is smooth and quick.

4. If any of the criteria above are not met, you may have a problem, and it's recommended you refer it to a bike shop mechanic.

SUSPENSION FORK MAINTENANCE

For this work, refer to the instruction manual that came with the

specific fork. In addition to cleaning, you may be able to adjust one or more of the following:

- preload, which controls the response rate, i.e. how easy it is to compress the fork;

- damping, i.e. how much it see-saws up and down after compression and release;

- travel, i.e. how far the fork can go down and back up again (this can only be adjusted by opening the fork and replacing its internal parts, and only on certain models;

- rebound rate, i.e. how quickly it recovers after compression.

On different forks, there may be different methods and locations for making these adjustments, mainly depending on the type of spring elements used.

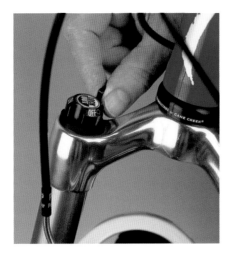

Above: Fig. 22.7. A lever on top of some forks allows locking out the suspension.

Left: Fig. 22.6. Preload adjustment.

Right: Fig. 22.8. Rebound adjustment at the bottom of the slider tube.

TRAVEL AND PRELOAD CHECK

The manufacturer's fact sheet (provided with the fork or available on the Web) states the maximum amount of travel a fork has. To get the maximum benefit from that fork, you need to set it up so that you actually use as much of that available travel as possible. To do that, first measure what I call the "active travel," i.e. the amount of compression you achieve under normal riding conditions.

TOOLS & EQUIPMENT:

- zip-tie

- calipers

PROCEDURE:

1. Strap the zip-tie tightly around the stanchion tube and push it up against the top of the slider tube.

2. Sit on the bike, distributing your weight the same way as you would riding it. This is the

passive load and the zip-tie will be pushed down some distance.

3. Get off again and measure the distance between the zip-tie and the top of the slider tube. This distance should be no more than 25 percent of the total available travel (for example, it should not be more than 15 mm on a fork with 60 mm nominal travel).

4. Go for a 30-minute ride in the most demanding terrain you would typically ride. The zip-tie gets pushed up further, and the distance between it

and the top of the slider is the fork's active travel. It should be close to the maximum quoted. In fact, it's about right if just once or twice during a demanding ride, you feel the fork bottoming out.

Above: Fig. 22.10. Measuring active travel range after ride

Left: Fig. 22.9. Using Zip-tie to mark inactive position of stanchion relative to the top of the slider tube.

Right: Fig. 22.11. A different type of suspension: Sophisticated linkage fork on small-wheel Alex Moulton full-suspension bike.

ACTIVE TRAVEL & PRELOAD ADJUSTMENT

Referring to the information supplied with the fork in question, locate the preload adjuster (usually on top of each stanchion). Turn it to reduce the preload to the lowest value. Then check the ride to see whether it bottoms out on rebound. If it does, adjust the preload up a little. This will give you the maximum amount of effective travel.

23

REAR SUSPENSION MAINTENANCE

Although traditionally rear suspension was mainly used on downhill mountain bikes, it's now also penetrating other market segments. Several manufacturers even offer city bikes with suspension.

REAR SUSPENSION SYSTEMS

As with front suspension, there are a number of different ways to achieve suspension of the rear end of the bike.

For the common terminology and general concepts that are common to all forms of suspension, refer to Chapter 22, where they were described in conjunction with front suspension technology. Unfortunately, the more sophisticated, the more troublesome the rear suspension is likely to be. The most sophisticated ones, such as those used on downhill mountain bikes, tend to have many linkages and pivot points, which all add up to potential loose connections, due to wear after some use.

From a maintenance standpoint, there are two important things to watch, and they're common on all those different types: the shock unit itself and the pivot points where the different linkage elements rotate relative to the frame and/or each other.

Above and right: Figs. 23.1 and 23.2. Two of the many different ways to provide rear suspension on a mountain bike.

If you don't want to get more involved in rear suspension maintenance, at least keep all these parts clean, and regularly lubricate the pivot points, using a non-greasy lubricant. Wipe off any excess lubricant. Also tighten the pivot bolts once a month.

SUSPENSION SEATPOSTS

Some relevant words about these remarkably simple and effective devices are included in Chapter 20, which deals with general seat and seatpost issues. But don't combine a suspension seatpost with a "real" rear suspension.

SHOCK UNIT MAINTENANCE

The heart of any rear suspension system is a shock unit, comprising the spring element and a damping device. The spring element may be an external coil spring or an air

cartridge. The damping device is usually in the form of an oil cylinder with a piston with valves through which the oil flows as the piston is displaced.

In addition to regularly cleaning the shock unit once a month and after each ride in wet or dusty terrain, inspect the unit once a month. If there are any traces of oil, it means the unit leaks and should be replaced.

Replacing it involves the same work as described below for a seasonal inspection. Remove the rear wheel before starting this work.

TOOLS & EQUIPMENT:

- Allen wrench to fit pivot bolt

- open-ended wrench to fit pivot nut

- cleaning cloths

MAINTENANCE PROCEDURE:

1. At the front end of the shock unit (where it is attached to

the main frame), unscrew the pivot bolt while holding the nut at the other end.

2. Also undo the pivot bolt in the back (where the unit is attached to the rear triangle).

3. Check the rear triangle (which is now free to move) for any looseness or rough rotation of the pivots. If so, disassemble, clean, lubricate, and/or replace pivot bushings or bearings.

Above: Fig. 23.5. Inflating a pneumatic cartridge of an air-oil shock unit.

Above and right: Figs. 23.3 and 23.4. Two more mountain bike suspension systems. Fig. 23.4 is Alex Moulton's solution.

4. Clean and lightly oil exposed parts of the shock unit. Replace if defective.

5. If it's an air-sprung unit that's been losing air pressure, replace the air valve (usually a standard bicycle valve), and reinflate to the specified pressure.

6. Reassemble in reverse sequence. Replace the locking-insert nuts used on the shock unit mounting bolts by new ones.

SUSPENSION TROUBLESHOOTING

Here's a short list of the most common suspension problems and their solutions. These points

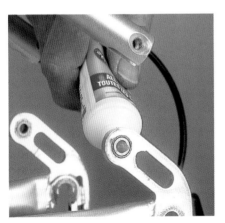

apply both to front and rear suspension.

Problem: Suspension dips even on minor bumps and often bottoms out.

Cause/Solution: The spring is too weak. If air-sprung, increase air pressure. Otherwise, replace the coil spring or the elastomer pads by higher rated ones.

Problem: Suspension not responsive enough.

Cause/Solution: The spring is too stiff. If air-sprung, reduce air pressure. Otherwise, replace spring element by a lower rated one.

Problem: Suspension sags more and more as the ride progresses.

Cause/Solution: Insufficient recovery, or rebound. Adjust the re-

Above: Fig. 23.8. Checking pivots.

Top left: Fig. 23.6. Lubricating the main pivot bearing with grease nipple.

Bottom left: Fig. 23.7. Lubricating the linkage pivot bearing bushes.

Right: Fig. 23.9. Adjusting the preload.

bound adjuster until the bike absorbs fast, repetitive impacts without loss of stability.

Problem: Suspension stiffens up progressively as the ride progresses.

Cause/Solution: Too much compression stage damping. Adjust for less compression stage damping.

Problem: Unequal responsiveness between front and rear suspension.

Cause/Solution: Non-compatible spring elements front and rear. Choose fork and rear shock with similar amounts of travel. Whereas it's fixed in the rear, you may be able to replace the front fork elements by ones with more (or less) travel.

Problem: Unpredictable behavior of rear end of the bike while turning.

Cause/Solution: Remove the shock unit and check for resistance. If it feels too soft, have it overhauled or replaced.

24
LIGHTING EQUIPMENT MAINTENANCE

Nighttime cycling no longer has to be the dangerous undertaking it was considered to be some 20 years ago. Today, excellent lighting systems and individual lights—both front and rear—are readily available at most bike shops.

LIGHTING SYSTEMS

There are four general types of bicycle lights in use today:

- battery lights with built-in batteries in the light unit;

- battery lights with separate, central battery;

- generator (dynamo) lights;

- hybrid systems using a generator and a battery back-up.

In the U.S. and England, battery lighting is used almost exclusively, while generator lighting is more common on the European continent.

From a practical standpoint, generator lighting should be taken more seriously than it usually is. Its great advantage is that it's always available when you need it—no need to make sure the batteries are charged or that you have proper spares with you. That's especially important for those who use their bikes frequently but not only for fixed-schedule commuting. The following sections contain de-

Left: Fig. 24.1. Front halogen bulb light with separate frame-mounted battery.

Right: Fig. 24.2. Modern powerful LED front light with built in battery.

tailed maintenance information on all available types of lighting systems.

LIGHTS WITH BUILT-IN BATTERIES

In the front, these usually clamp directly or indirectly to the handlebars, or in England often to a clip on the fork. In the rear, they attach either to the seatpost or e.g. to a luggage rack or the seatstays. The one used for the front should be bright and produce a compact bundle of light that should be aimed at an area of the road about 20–30 feet (6–9 m) in front of the bike. Usually, there's a clamp that stays on the handlebars once installed and the light just slides and clips into this clamp, so you can remove it when you leave the bike unguarded.

The one for the rear should be red, and point straight back (neither up nor down, neither left nor right). The rear light does not need to be quite so bright as the one in front. LEDs (Light Emit-

ting Diodes) appear to be very suitable for this use, mainly because they provide much longer battery life. The LEDs themselves also last much longer than light bulbs—however, they don't last forever either, and the light should be replaced if they, or individual LEDs in a multi-LED array, become dim.

The most common maintenance required on battery lights is replacing the batteries and the bulbs. A battery charge typically lasts less than 4 hours, so it's a good idea to carry spares (and especially if you use rechargeable ones, recharge them at least once a month). Before you go on a longer ride that may take you into darkness (even if not planned), check the condition of both the batteries in the light and the spare batteries.

If you use rechargeable batteries, note the difference between the two most common types of lights. As rechargeable replacement batteries for standard-size cells, only NiCad (Nickel-Cadmium) and NiMH (Nickel-Metal-Hydride) are available. NiMH batteries last considerably longer but are much more expensive. However, they're worth the price because they also have a longer shelf life (i.e. they will hold a charge much longer when not used).

Bulbs typically don't last more than about 100 hours of use. Get some spare bulbs and carry one for each light on the bike, e.g. in the tire patch kit. If

Above: Fig. 24.4. Modern LED battery rear light.

Left: Fig. 24.3. Conventional handlebar-mounted battery light, opened up to expose batteries and bulb contacts.

Top right: Fig. 24.5. Seatpost-mounted LED rear light.

Bottom right: Fig. 24.6. Flashing LED rear light opened up to expose batteries and circuitry.

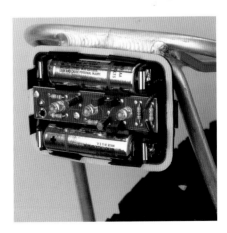

you use the nice bright halogen bulbs, don't touch the glass with your bare hands, because the acidity will etch the glass dull, reducing their light output once they get hot.

In recent years, there has been significant development in the field of LED lights. LEDs with outputs of 1 Watt and even more challenge all but the most powerful halogen lights. A 1 Watt LED is about as powerful as a 3 Watt halogen light, resulting in increased battery light. Less powerful LEDs also have their place, especially for rear lights. In flashing mode, their batteries will last 100 hours or more (less when burning constantly, but still much longer than with standard bulbs)—and they are more visible in flashing mode.

LIGHTS WITH CENTRAL BATTERY

These lights are typically more powerful and often have high beam and low beam capabilities. Their larger battery, consisting of

several cells wired up together, is either packaged in a pouch tied to the bike or neatly packed away in something that fits in a water bottle cage (actually, a real water bottle is often used, with the battery cells inserted and the space around them filled with some kind of compound to keep everything in place).

Again, the batteries and the bulbs need to be checked and replaced if necessary (although the batteries are almost always rechargeable, in which case you just plug the unit in via its recharging adapter, which should do the trick in about 2 hours). In addition to NiCad and NiMH batteries, there are also lead-acid gel batteries. The latter require different care: they have to be recharged *before* they are fully discharged, i.e. before the light gets dim, whereas the other types seem to last longest if they are drained completely before they are recharged. See the preceding section *Battery Lights With Built-In Battery* for more in-

formation regarding spare bulbs and batteries.

In addition to bulbs and batteries, there is wiring to deal with. So, if the light doesn't work and you've checked the bulb and the battery, and found them to be OK, check the wiring. Usually it's a connection at the end of the wiring, so check there first and fix it with a soldering iron and solder. If there are any exposed metal wire parts, use electrical insulating tape to fix it. You may have to replace the wiring completely if you can't identify the source of the problem.

GENERATOR LIGHTS

This type also has a central power source and wiring connecting it to the light—actually it usually feeds both a front light and a rear light. Usually, the electricity is carried by a single wire and returned to the generator via the metal of the bike, for which purpose each part—generator, front light, and rear light—has a pinch-screw to make what's called a mass con-

Fig. 24.7. Light system with central battery.

Above: Fig. 24.8. Wiring connection on light system with frame-mounted battery.

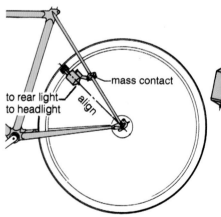

Fig. 24.9. Generator alignment.

tact. It is also possible (and less trouble-prone) to use two-pole wiring instead of relying on mass contacts. In that case, the connections are made with little two-prong plugs and sockets.

The safest place for the generator is on the rear wheel, where accidental loosening does not impose the risk of a serious accident as much as it does in the front. Even so, keep it tightened properly. It should be mounted so that the longitudinal centerline points to the center of the hub.

Here too, the most common problem, other than burned-out

bulbs, is wiring failure. Especially the point where the wires connect to the dynamo is subject to accidental disconnection. Check it frequently and be careful to route your wire in such a way that it isn't likely to get caught when e.g. storing or parking the bike.

There are two generator-specific problems: slip and mass connections.

- To prevent slip, which is most common in wet weather, make sure the generator is aligned as shown in Fig. 24.9, and with the roller running on a rubber part of the tire, rather than the almost

bare sidewall of a skinny tire on the one hand or the thick "knobbies" on a mountain bike tire on the other.

- Mass connections are pinch screws that connect one side of the lights and of the generator to the metal of the bike's frame. They sometimes don't make a good contact, and you can restore the contact by loosening ant re-tightening the pinch screws.

BOTTOM BRACKET GENERATORS

Bottom-bracket-mounted generators rub against the rear tire from underneath the chainstays. Being

Fig. 24.10. Light system with central battery.

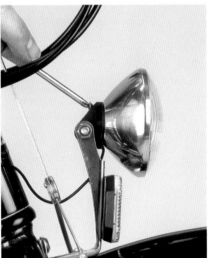

Above: Fig. 24.12. Opening up front light to replace bulb or to check contact connection.

Left: Fig. 24.11. Replacing halogen bulb: Don't touch the glass of the bulb.

Top right: Fig. 24.13. Luggage-rack mounted rear light and reflector.

Bottom right: Fig. 24.14. Replacing rear light bulb.

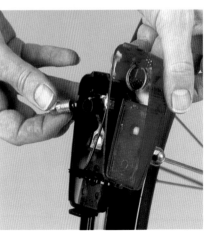

mounted in the messiest place on any bike, they are notorious for slippage problems in wet weather. You can increase the spring force by tying a little bungee cord between the roller mount and a fixed point on the bike close to the rear wheel axle.

HUB GENERATORS

Hub generators are a very nice solution to typical generator problems. Built into the front wheel, these devices not only aren't subject to slipping, they are also more efficient than regular tire-driven generators. They do cause a little extra drag (barely perceptible) when the light is not switched on. When the light is turned on, they have significantly

less drag than any conventional generators.

- The whole front wheel has to be rebuilt around them. Unfortunately, they're also quite a bit more expensive.

SYSTEMATIC TROUBLESHOOTING

If a lighting system with central battery or generator does not work properly, proceed systematically in finding out what's wrong and correcting any problems found. Follow the steps outlined in the troubleshooting diagram Fig. 24.15.

For lights with a central battery, the most important advice is to make sure the battery is fully

charged before any trip that may involve night-time riding. You may even consider carrying a small light with built-in batteries as a spare light source in case of problems with the light.

Generators often slip in wet weather. The problem can be minimized by bending the mounting hardware in to the point where the unengaged position leaves only about 6 mm (¼ in.) between the roller and the tire. Another solution is to put a smooth rubber cap around the roller.

Above: Fig. 24.16. Hub generator, built into the front wheel.

Below: Fig. 24.17. Bottom bracket generator, viewed from underneath the chainstays.

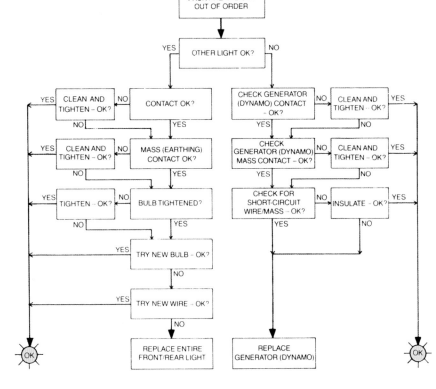

Fig. 24.15. Troubleshooting diagram for system with central generator or battery

25

ACCESSORY MAINTENANCE

An accessory, as opposed to a component, is defined as any part that is, or can be, installed on the bike but is not part of its essential operation. In this chapter, we'll deal with the most common accessories other than lights, which were covered in Chapter 24.

ACCESSORY TYPES

Thousands of accessories have been introduced for bicycle use at different times, and hundreds are still available today. What they all have in common is some kind of attachment to the bike. And that's indeed the most common maintenance problem of all components. In addition, there will be some more specific advice concerning the most important and/or common accessories in use today:

- lock
- pump
- bicycle computer
- luggage racks

- fenders
- kick stand
- reflectors

GENERAL ACCESSORY COMMENTS

The two tenets of accessory maintenance are:

- keep it tightly mounted
- replace (or remove) it if it's broken

Left: Fig. 25.1. Fully accessorized city bike. Complete with lights, bell, racks with bags, fenders with mudflap, chain guard, kickstand, and a built-in lock.

Right: Fig. 25.2. Close-up of lock, generator, and rack attachment detail.

The last thing you want on the bike is an accessory that hangs loose and/or doesn't do its job. Check the installation hardware regularly, tightening all nuts, bolts, and clamps. And by all means, remove the item if it doesn't work and you haven't been able to fix it. Before replacing it in that case, ask yourself whether you could do without it altogether, and don't replace it unless the answer is no.

Generally, any attachment hardware should have at least two mounting bolts, so vibration is less likely to rattle it loose. Another thing to watch out for is that items clamped around another part of the bike should fit snugly. Preferably there should be a flexible plastic or rubber protective sleeve around the bicycle component, which helps protect the bike's finish and aids in keeping the accessory mounting hardware in place.

LOCK

There's not much maintenance required on this, unfortunately, most essential accessory. Lubrication is done once or twice a year by inserting the nozzle of a thin lubricant, such as WD-40, at the point where the bolt enters into the lock mechanism and spraying in just a tiny little squirt of oil. In addition, you can put some oil on the key, insert it in the lock, and then close and open the lock 2 or 3 times to lubricate it. If your lock can be attached to the bike frame, check and tighten the bolts of the clamp that holds it during the monthly inspection.

PUMP

I suggest you use two kinds of pumps: a floor pump for at home and a frame-mounted hand pump for on the road. Once or twice a year, tighten the screw cap at the head. If the pump doesn't work, first take the head apart. Sometimes you can get by with turning the flexible grommet (that's a thick washer) around, or you may have to replace it.

The other item that sometimes gives trouble is the rubber or plastic plunger inside the barrel. It can be reached by unscrewing the cap at the point where the plunger mechanism enters the barrel. Flex it, knead it, apply some lubricant to it, and if you can't get it to work, you'll probably have to replace the

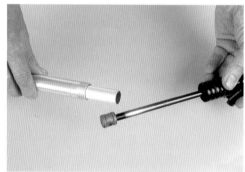

Above: Fig. 25.5. Small pump taken apart to expose the flexible plunger.

Top left: Fig. 25.3. Keep all accessories firmly mounted.

Bottom left: Fig. 25.4. Lubricating the lock at the key.

Top right: Fig. 25.6. Pump detail of valve-fitting parts.

Bottom right: Fig. 25.7. Installing bicycle computer.

entire pump, unless you can find a replacement.

BICYCLE COMPUTER

Bicycle computers have also improved dramatically over time. Even so, they're still fidgety items.

Check the installation of the pickup that's attached to a spoke, and the matching sensor, to make sure they pass each other closely. Check the condition of the wire, and tie it down at intermediate points with zip-ties or electric insulating tape so they don't get caught or damaged. And again, if it doesn't work, replace or discard the entire system, computer, mounting bracket, sensor, pick-up, wire, and all.

Wireless models are available now. Though not necessarily trouble-free either, they're certainly "tidier" without all the wires hanging loose on your bike.

LUGGAGE RACK

Luggage racks, or carriers, are available both for the front and the rear. Although the rear is the most common place for heavy and bulky items, a well-mounted front rack can help stabilize the bike if it has to be heavily loaded. For the installation of racks, it's preferable if the frame and the front fork have brazed-on bosses and eyelets at the dropouts and fork ends to attach the rack to.

If there are no bosses and eyelets, you can install clips around the fork and the stays (providing it's not a super light-weight bike, on which the material might get damaged by the force on the clip). Especially at the fork, which has tapered fork blades (thicker at the top, tapering to thinner near the bottom), there is a risk of the clips slipping down. Mount a rubber or flexible plastic sleeve between the clip and the bike, and frequently check the connections (daily on a loaded tour), tightening them firmly.

FENDERS

Both during and after rainfall, fenders (mud guards) help keep water and mud off the bike, the rider, and those following behind.

Above: Fig. 25.9. Quick-release mount detail of the same rack.

Top left: Fig. 25.10. Safety fender stay mounts: they disengage when forced.

Bottom left: Fig. 25.8. Seatpost-mounted rack with bag-mounting rails, straps, and reflector.

Center right: Fig. 25.11. Top fender mounting detail.

Bottom right: Fig. 25.12. Fender stay attachment.

Again, make sure they're firmly connected at the various mounting points. Also check to make sure they don't rub against the tire or another moving part.

If the fenders and their mounting hardware are not very rigid which is often the case, at least the one in the front should have a clip that will come loose if the fender gets caught in the wheel, so as to prevent a serious accident due to the front wheel locking up. Just the same, check the connections regularly and tighten the hardware—or discard the fender if you can't get it tight enough.

At the bottom of the front fender, it's a good idea to install a flexible mud flap, which keeps splashing water off your feet and the lower part of the bike. Since they are rarely available in U.S. bike shops, you can make one yourself from any flexible material, whether it's a piece cut off a discarded plastic water bottle or a piece of the uppers of an old rubber boot. Drill 6 mm (¼ in.) holes in the bottom of the fender and in the top of the flap, and attach the flap to the mudguard

with a set of 5 mm bolts, nuts, and washers.

CHAIN GUARD

To protect the chain from foul weather and dirt, only a fully-enclosed chain guard will do the trick. This type is only available on city bikes without derailleur. Open chain guards serve only to protect clothing, and are easy to install as an after-market item.

WATER BOTTLE CAGE

Keep the water bottle cage attachment bolts tightened. If the bike does not have threaded bosses for a water bottle cage,

Left: Fig. 25.13. Mud flap at bottom of the fender.

Top right: Fig. 25.15. Installing an open chain guard.

Bottom right: Fig. 25.16. Installing a water bottle cage.

Below: Fig. 25.14. Removable panel on a fully enclosed chain guard to gain access to the chain and the sprocket.

you can get one with clips that fit around the down tube.

KICK STAND

Also called prop stand, this device is found mainly on low-end bikes. On a frame that's properly designed for its use, it can be an OK item, because there's a flat plate to which it is bolted with either a 10 mm Allen bolt or a regular hexagonal bolt. To accommodate different bike types, the kick stand should be adjustable (though woefully few are).

If the frame was not designed for installation of a kick stand, it is usually clamped around the chainstays just forward of the bridge piece that connects them.

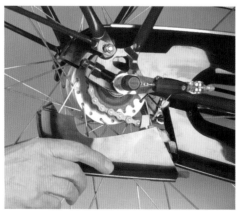

My advice is to remove it, because it tends to come loose, twist around, and damage the chainstay. However, if you must have one on your bike, at least tighten it once a month—or try to find the type that is clamped on at the rear wheel axle. An acceptable kick stand is the one that mounts close to the rear wheel axle, with a clamp that attaches it both to the chainstay and the seatstay.

WARNING DEVICES

Either a bell, a horn, or a whistle will alert others to your presence, but only the first will identify you as a cyclist. As for installation and maintenance of a bell, mount it within easy reach and keep the mounting bolt tight. If there's a metal mechanism inside, give it a drop of oil once a month.

REFLECTORS

The law in the U.S. and most other Western countries requires bicycles to be equipped with a number of reflectors when used at night. These are not just gadgets but real safety items, and you really need them in the dark (not just at night: they're just as essential e.g. in a tunnel). But don't think they're adequate substitutes for lights in night-time cycling—see Chapter 24 for information on lights.

Make sure the reflectors are mounted firmly and point straight back (for the one in the rear) or forward (for the one in the front).

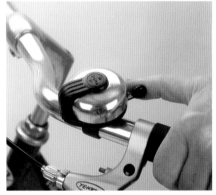

Although the one in the back can give adequate protection against following motorists, never solely rely on the one in front—get a front light instead. Lights are more visible over a wider angle of coverage for all directions from which you may be endangered *and* they allow you to see where you're going yourself.

Replace any reflector that is cracked or broken, because water can enter through the crack and "fog up" the reflective pattern on the inside of the lens, making it "blind."

Above: Fig. 25.18. Install the bell so it can be reached without moving your hand.

Left: Fig. 25.17. Checking the kickstand mounting bolt.

Top right: Fig. 25.19. Installing a front reflector.

Bottom right: Fig. 25.20. Installing a rear reflector on a luggage rack.

Appendix: Tools Overview

Most bicycle maintenance and repair operations require the use of some tools. Although it is possible to spend several thousand dollars on a complete workshop, you should be able to carry out most jobs with a relatively modest assortment. That will at least get you started, and as you begin to handle more complicated jobs, you can buy specific additional tools as the need arises.

Types of Tools

The two types of tools are general tools, found in any good hardware store, and bicycle-specific tools, available only in bike stores. Here you will find a description of the most common and essential tools, as well as those used for specific jobs described in this book.

When buying tools, it's very important not to skimp: choose the highest quality available. Not only are good tools more accurate, they also are stronger. Although initially they'll be a lot more expensive than similar-looking "economy" tools, they'll actually turn out to be more economical in the long run because they will provide lasting service without damaging the bicycle or its components.

Equally important is to select tools of the correct size: If they don't fit snugly, they're the wrong size, and that too might lead to damage, both to the part your working on and the tool itself.

Basic Tool Set

Before describing the intricacies of the many different tools for bicycle use, I suggest you buy a small selection of tools that will serve you well for the first few jobs (and indeed for most jobs you'll encounter). This is also the set of tools you should carry with you on any long bike trip (and for that purpose, get a pouch to hold them that can be attached to the bike, e.g. under the saddle. You can buy these tools at any bike shop, where some of them will be available together in a set (in fact, you may find a set containing almost all of them together, neatly wrapped up in a pouch). Here's a list of what should be included:

- tire pump with a fitting suitable for the type of valves used on your bike's tires

- tire pressure gauge, also for the type of valves used

- set of 3 tire levers

- tire patch kit (patches, adhesive, and sandpaper or scraper)

- set of metric Allen wrenches (Allen keys) in sizes 4, 5, and 6 mm

- a flat-head and a Phillips-head screwdriver

- small adjustable wrench

- spoke wrench (nipple spanner) to fit the spoke nipples on the wheels of your bike

- crank tools, at least the one for tightening the bolt that holds the crank to the bottom bracket axle (on many new bikes that means just a fitting Allen wrench)

- small can of spray lubricant

- cloth for cleaning

- tube of waterless hand-cleaning paste

Detailed descriptions of the individual items listed above are contained in the following sections dealing with general and bike-specific tools respectively.

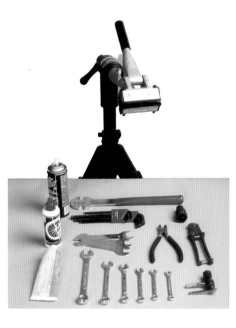

Left: Fig. A.1. Set of essential tools, both as the basis of your workshop and to take along on any bike trip.

Right: Fig. A.2. Collection of tools and a repair stand.

GENERAL TOOLS

These are the common tools (as opposed to bicycle-specific tools) that can be purchased at any general tool or hardware shop. Note though, that most bicycle components are built to metric standards, and therefore the tools will generally have to be for metric sizes, i.e. measured in mm (millimeters). This even applies to most American-made machines.

Often tools are available in the form of combination tools. Although this may be convenient for items to take with you on the bike, in general I've found individual tools more convenient to use. On the other hand, it's a good idea to buy tools in sets, because generally a set of different-sized wrenches is likely to be cheaper than it would be to buy them separately.

ALLEN WRENCHES

Called Allen keys in the U.K., these L-shaped hexagonal rods are needed for the currently common bolts with a hexagonal recess in the head. They are identified by their across-flat dimension, corresponding to the size of the recess in which they fit. Get them in sizes from 2 mm to 10 mm to cover all possible bicycle-relevant applications.

OPEN-ENDED, BOX, & COMBINATION WRENCHES

These tools are used on hexagon-headed bolts and nuts, and other items with parallel flat exterior surfaces, primarily if you have access to them from the side. The combination wrench is called so because it combines an open-ended wrench at one end with a box wrench (ring spanner) on the other. They are also designated by their across-flat dimension, corresponding to the dimension of the nut or bolt head on which they fit. Get two sets in sizes from 7 mm through 17 mm. The two other types mentioned here can also be used, although they are not as convenient as their combination version.

SOCKET WRENCHES

These are also used for hexagon-headed bolts and nuts, mainly for those to which you only have access from the end (rather than the side). Usually sold in sets consisting of one or more levers or handles (often with a ratchet mechanism) and sockets with

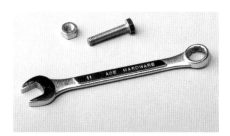

hexagon recesses in the end in several different sizes. You may need them in sizes from 7 through 17 mm.

ADJUSTABLE WRENCHES

This tool is similar to the open-ended wrench but is adjustable for different across-flat sizes. Most practical are the ones referred to as Crescent wrenches in the U.S. (where that was originally a brand name). They are usually designated by their overall length. A longer wrench can be used on bigger bolts than a smaller one. You will need a 6-inch and a 10-inch one to handle practically any size nut or bolt used on a bicycle. Since it's better to use non-adjustable tools, because they tend to fit more accurately, I suggest getting only one of each and relying on combination wrenches and/or socket wrenches as much as possible, resorting to the adjustable wrench only when nothing else fits.

SCREWDRIVERS

Most convenient for bicycle use are relatively short, stubby ones. Get a small, a medium, and a large one each of the regular straight-blade and the Phillips head (cross-head) variety. For bicycle

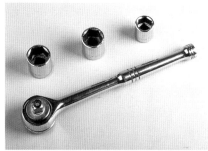

Above: Fig. A.4. Combination wrench (open-ended wrench and ring wrench) and hexagonal-head bolt and nut.

Left: Fig. A.3. Multi-tool and individual Allen wrenches, with inset showing Bondus type Allen wrench tip.

Top right: Fig. A.5. Socket wrench set.

Bottom right: Fig. A.6. Crescent-type adjustable wrench.

use, small is 3–4 mm wide for the straight-blade screwdriver, medium is about 5–7 mm, and large is 8–10 mm.

NEEDLE-NOSE PLIERS

These tools are sometimes needed to pull a cable or a wire taut or to get hold of small items by clamping them in. If available in different sizes, get a relatively small one.

DIAGONAL CUTTERS

These tools may be needed to cut through something like a wire or a cable casing. Again, a relatively small one will probably serve you best.

HAMMERS & MALLETS

Yes, even for such simple tools there's sometimes a use in bicycle mechanics. They're referenced by their weight. Get a relatively light metal-working hammer (about 300–400 g, or 10–14 oz.) and a small plastic mallet of about the same weight.

FILES

Sometimes used to clean up parts with a sharp burr or items you have cut off, you'll find a use for a small half-round file, about 10 in (25 cm) long including the handle, and a similarly sized flat file, and both must be of the type designed for metal work.

SAWS

This is yet another simple item that should not be frequently used in bicycle repair. It must be designed for metal work, and I prefer the handy small one often referred to as an Eclipse saw.

TORX WRENCHES

Shaped like Allen wrenches, but with star-shaped ends, these are used on very shallow-headed bolts, primarily used to attach brake disks to the (special) hubs. They are also available in the form of screwdrivers.

TORQUE WRENCHES

A torque wrench is recommended for use on some sensitive components, such as those of the suspension system to avoid overtightening them. The manufacturers of such components list the maximum torque (think of it as the force applied by the tool in tightening) in Nm (Newton-meter) or ft-lb foot-pound).

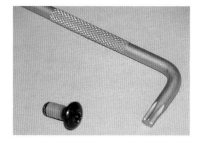

Above: Fig. A.8. Torx wrench and Torx bolt.

Left: Fig. A.7. Diagonal cutters and needle-nose pliers.

Top right: Fig. A.9. Calipers.

Bottom right: Fig. A.10. Torque wrench.

MEASURING EQUIPMENT

Buy a simple measuring tape, a 30 or 45 cm metal straightedge (ruler) with mm markings, and a pair of calipers (vernier gauge). The calipers should have both metric and inch readings, because although most of the bike's nuts and bolts are to metric standards, some other parts are made to inch sizes (e.g. the headset and the bottom bracket).

BICYCLE-SPECIFIC TOOLS

The catalogues of bicycle tool supply companies contain literally hundreds of different tools, of which only a limited number are essential for the type of work you're likely to carry out yourself. (Many of the others are used to speed up specific jobs encountered at a bike shop but are not essential). This section contains descriptions of only the most commonly used bicycle-specific tools, all of which can be bought at most good bike shops.

Some of these tools may be specific for a particular make or model of the relevant bike component it is to be used for. The descriptions point that

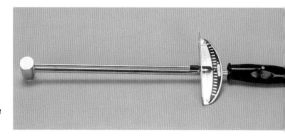

out wherever that may be the case. I suggest you take the bike to the shop where you buy the tools to make sure you get the appropriate version of such tools.

PUMP

In addition to the small pump that can be carried on the bike, you'll probably find a larger floor pump very convenient, because it allows you to inflate tires much faster and with less effort. Make sure the "head" (the fitting that goes on the valve) matches the kind of valves used on your bike, although you can buy an adaptor to switch from one type to the other. If you work on different bikes with different types of valves, it's not a bad idea to actually have a pump for each type, because it can be a hassle to switch adaptors on the pump.

PRESSURE GAUGE

This item shows the pressure to which the tires are inflated much more reliably than you can gauge it by pushing the tire in with your thumb. Although many floor pumps have one built in, I

much prefer to use one that can be carried around. Make sure it matches the type of valve used on your tires.

TIRE LEVERS

These tools are used to lift the tires off the rim in order to repair or replace either the tire or the inner tube. Sold in sets of three, you should insist on thin, flat ones. Only use them for tire removal, not to install the tire (Chapter 5 explains how to do that without using a tool).

TIRE REPAIR KIT (PATCH KIT)

This is usually sold in a little box containing adhesive patches, rubber solution (adhesive cement), and a piece of sandpaper or a scraper to roughen the area to be repaired. The little box can also be used to store other small parts.

CRANK TOOL

On many bikes, tightening or removing the cranks requires a specific tool, be it

an oversize Allen wrench or a special socket wrench. Check with the bike shop which is appropriate for your particular bike.

SPOKE WRENCH

Called nipple spanner in the U.K., this tool is used to install, remove, or adjust the tension of spokes. They are available both in single units with several different-sized cutouts (for the different nipple sizes you may encounter) and as separate tools each for only one nipple size. I suggest you shy away from multiple-size ones, since they are confusing. Only use an accurately fitting one, because you're likely to ruin the nipple if the cutout is larger than the across-flat dimension of the nipple.

CHAIN TOOL

This tool is used to push one of the pins (partially) out of, and back into, the chain to allow the removal, installation, lengthening, or shortening of the chain. Some chains (specifically those marketed by Shimano under the designation Hyperglide) require a very specific version of this tool, so make sure the tool you buy matches your chain—I suggest you buy both a Hyperglide tool and a general one for all other chains.

PEDAL WRENCH

This is a long, relatively thin, flat open-ended wrench that fits between the pedal and the crank. It has a long

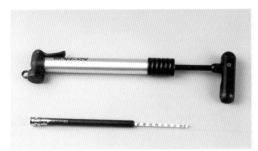

Above: Fig. A.13. Crank tools. The top one is self-contained, while the other one is used in conjunction with a wrench.

Top left: Fig. A.11. Tire patch kit and tire levers.

Bottom left: Fig. A.12. Pump and tire pressure gauge.

Bottom right: Fig. A.14. Spoke wrenches.

handle for adequate leverage to remove the pedals from the crank. There are several sizes, most bikes requiring either $9/16$ inch or 15 mm.

CONE WRENCHES

Cone wrenches are thin open-ended wrenches used to adjust, remove, or install the bearings on wheel hubs. They usually come with two different sizes on either end of the tool, and I suggest getting two each of whatever it takes to cover the size range from 13 through 17 mm.

CABLE CUTTERS

Although diagonal cutters can be used to cut control cables, these tools will give a cleaner cut, with less chance of frayed strands.

FREEWHEEL TOOLS

These are used to remove either the screwed-on freewheel mechanism from a rear wheel hub with separate screwed-on freewheel or to disassemble the set of cogs on a cassette-type rear hub. Get one that fits the particular freewheel or cassette on your bike.

CHAIN WHIPS AND COG WRENCHES

These are tools that are used in pairs to separate the cogs on a bike with a screwed-on freewheel. They can also be used singly for bikes with cassette freewheels to restrain the freewheel when unscrewing the cog set.

BOTTOM BRACKET TOOLS

to work on the bottom bracket, you may need either one or several special tools, depending on the type, make, and model of the bottom bracket. Usu-

Above: Fig. A.17. Cable cutters. More accurate than diagonal cutters for cutting inner and outer control cables.

Top left: Fig. A.15. Hyperglide and regular chain tools.

Bottom left: Fig. A.16. Cone wrenches.

Right: Fig. A.20. Wheel building tools: truing stand, spoke-tension gauge, and centering gauge.

Below: Figs. A.18 and A.19. Sprocket removal tools. The tools to remove threaded freewheels and cartridge bottom bracket bearings are similar.

ally, though, you'll need at least a large flat crescent-shaped wrench with one or more prongs for the lockring and a pin wrench for the bearing cup, while the other bearing cup may require a different type of flat wrench.

HEADSET TOOLS

These are thin open-ended wrenches, designed to fit the parts of the threaded headset bearings. If your bike has a threaded headset, these tools will be needed for any headset adjusting and maintenance work, as well as to remove or install the front fork. They are specific to the make, model, and size of headset installed on the bike in question.

OTHER TOOLS

There are many other bicycle-specific and general tools available, which you may want to buy if the specific job you encounter requires them. Ask at a bike shop what the tools cost versus their price for fixing your problem before you invest too much in fancy tools you may rarely use.

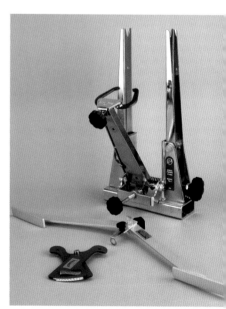

LUBRICANTS & CLEANING AIDS

Much maintenance work involves cleaning and lubricating various parts. Here is a list of items used for that.

BEARING GREASE

For the ball bearings on your bike, any make of bearing grease will do the job. Get one that's available in a tube, to avoid contamination of the grease.

MINERAL OIL

SAE 60 motor oil or any synthetic oil of similar thickness will be suitable to lubricate items that are not accessible for grease application. Even if you buy it in a can or a large bottle, put the supply you use in a small plastic squeeze bottle with a narrow spout.

HYDRAULIC OIL

See chapter 16 for remarks about the types of oil that are used for hydraulically operated brakes (usually disk brakes). It is also used in some suspension units.

PENETRATING OIL

Although there are special oils that are even more specifically suited to loosening overly tight connections, you will probably find that a small spray can of WD-40 does the job adequately and can be used as a lubricant in hard-to-reach places as well.

ANTI-SEIZE LUBRICANT

A paste to use on sensitive screw-threaded items, especially those of relatively large diameter made of aluminum, such as the headset, the bottom bracket, the freewheel, and the pedals.

THREAD-LOCK COMPOUND

Most commonly known by the brand name Loctite, this is essentially an adhesive that gets applied to the type of screwed connections that might otherwise come loose too easily under the effect of vibrations when riding, such as those holding accessories on the bike. It's available in several different bonding strengths (in color-coded bottles), and for bike use, the one in the red bottle seems to work best.

SOLVENTS

It's best to use biodegradable solvents, such as those based on citrus oil.

WAX

Both bare metal surfaces and paint are best protected by applying wax. Any automotive wax will do the trick (don't use furniture wax).

METAL CLEANER

Use it sparingly if the bare metal of the bike's components won't return to a healthy shine any other way. Read the label to make sure it's suitable for aluminum and chrome-plated steel.

CLOTHS & BRUSHES

Buy a bundle of cleaning cloths and two or three different-size brushes as seems appropriate for cleaning the bike and its parts. Throw out any cloths that have picked up a lot of dirt, to avoid damage to the finish of bike and components, and wash out the brushes after each use.

CONTAINERS

Use a deep metal or plastic bowl, about 10 in. (25 cm) diameter, and a larger shallow container for cleaning small parts and catching drips respectively.

Above: Fig. A.22. Special brush for cleaning around and between freewheel cogs.

Left: Fig. A.21. Lubricants and cleaning aids.

Right: Fig. A.23. Small collection of spare parts to take along on a longer trip.

BIBLIOGRAPHY

Baird, Stewart. *Performance Cycling: The Scientific Way to Get the Most out of Your Bicycle.* San Francisco, CA: Van der Plas Publications, 2000.

Ballantine, Richard. *Richard's 21st-Century Bicycle Book.* Woodstock, NY: Overlook Press, 2001.

Barnett, John. *Barnett's Manual: Analysis and Procedures for Bike Mechanics.* 4th. Edn. Boulder, CO: VeloPress, 2001.

Berto, Frank. *The Dancing Chain: History and Development of the Derailleur Bicycle.* 2nd Edn. San Francisco, CA: Van der Plas Publications, 2005.

——. *Bicycling Magazine's Complete Guide to Upgrading Your Bicycle.* Emmaus, PA: Rodale Press, 1989.

Jones, Calvin. *The Big Blue Bicycle Maintenance Book.* St. Paul, MN: Park Tool Co. 2001.

Brandt, Jobst. *The Bicycle Wheel.* 3rd. Edn. Palo Alto, CA: Avocet, 1995.

Break It, Fix It, Ride It. (Compact Disk). Pittsford, NY: Break It, Fix It, Ride It, Inc., 2001.

Burrows, Mike. *Bicycle Design: Towards the Perfect Machine.* York (GB): Open Road / Seattle, WA: Alpenbooks, 2000.

Cole, Clarence, H. J. Glenn, John S. Allen. *Glenn's New Complete Bicycle Manual.* New York, NY: Crown Publishers, 1987.

Cuthberson, Tom. *Anybody's Bike Book.* Berkeley, CA: Ten-Speed Press, 1998.

DeLong, Fred: *DeLong's Guide to Bicycles and Bicycling: The Art and Science.* 2nd Edn. Radnor, PA: Chilton Books, 1978.

Downs, Todd. *The Bicycling Guide to Complete Bicycle Maintenance and Repair.* 5th. Edn. Emmaus, PA: Rodale Press, 2005.

Milson, Fred. Complete Bike Maintenance. Osceola, WI: MBI Publishing, 2003.

Oliver, Tony. *Touring Bikes: A Practical Guide.* Ramsbury (GB): Crowood Press, 1990.

Ries, Richard. *Building Your Perfect Bike: From Bare Frame to Personalized Superbike.* Osceola, WI: MBI Publishing, 1997.

Roegner, Thomas. Mountain Bike Maintenance and Repair. San Francisco, CA: Cycle Publishing, 2004.

Sutherland, Howard. *Sutherland's Handbook for Bicycle Mechanics.* 4th Edn. Berkeley, CA: Sutherland Publications, 2000.

Van der Plas, Rob. *The Bicycle Repair Book.* 2nd Edn. San Francisco, CA: Bicycle Books, 1993.

——. *Bicycle Technology: Understanding, Selecting, and Maintaining the Modern Bicycle and its Components.* San Francisco, CA: Bicycle Books, 1991.

——. *Mountain Bike Maintenance.* San Francisco, CA: Cycle Publishing, 2006.

——. *Road Bike Maintenance: Repairing and Maintaining the Modern Lightweight Bicycle.* Osceola, WI: MBI Publishing, 1996.

Zinn, Lennard. *Zinn and the Art of Mountain Bike Maintenance.* 4th Edn. Boulder, CO: VeloPress, 2005.

——. *Mountain Bike Performance Handbook.* Osceola, WI: MBI Publishing / Boulder, CO: VeloPress, 1998.

INDEX

See our website http://www.cyclepublishing.com for information on our other titles, or to purchase books